SHANKS

The
Life and Wars
of
General Nathan George Evans, C.S.A.

SHANKS

The Life and Wars of
General
Nathan George Evans, C.S.A.

JASON H. SILVERMAN
SAMUEL N. THOMAS JR.
BEVERLY D. EVANS IV

DA CAPO PRESS

Cataloging-in-Publication Data is available from the Library of Congress.

ISBN 0-306-81147-2

First edition, First printing.

Published by Da Capo Press
A Member of the Perseus Books Group
http://www.dacapopress.com

Da Capo Press books are available at special discounts for bulk purchases in the U.S. by corporations, institutions, and other organizations. For more information, please contact the Special Markets Department at the Perseus Books Group, 11 Cambridge Center, Cambridge, MA 02142, or call (800) 255-1514 or (617) 252-5298, or email j.mccrary@perseusbooks.com.

1 2 3 4 5 6 7 8 9—06 05 04 03 02

CONTENTS

Photo insert: after page 142

Yet again, for Susan and Alex, who are my life; and for my dear friends Tom Appleton, Bob Gorman, and Paul DuBois, who greatly enrich my life.

— J.H.S. —

For Roland, Jimmie, Arthur, and Athalie, my grandparents; they planted the seeds of pride in my heritage. I miss them dearly, but they are always with me.

— S.N.T. Jr. —

ACKNOWLEDGMENTS

W^e have always been amused by books whose acknowledgments go on for page after page naming so many people that it resembles a telephone book. To thank everyone is, in essence, to thank no one and we now delight in recognizing those people who truly made this volume possible. Thanks must first be offered to Gary Evans and his father, the late Beverly D. Evans IV, without whom this book, of course, could not have been written. No biography of Shanks Evans had ever been undertaken and without the Evans family support and cooperation, this volume would not have been realized as well. Beverly was the family historian of sorts and his collection and transcription of his great uncle's letters and reports greatly facilitated this project's success. We are proud to be joined by him on the title page of this book. His son Gary graciously and generously allowed us access to the general's papers and the family's photographs included herein. Gary's unqualified support for, and enthusiasm toward, our project is tremendously appreciated and we sincerely hope he is pleased with our efforts.

Diane Timmerman supplied her knowledge of "Vic" and the Gary family as well as other bits of information along the way. Dr. Charlie Peery, a true son of the South, was instrumental in furnishing us with information that expedited our research considerably. Jim Taylor, another fine Southern gentleman, has a unique knowledge and talent with period music and was a great source, as always, for a number of questions.

We wish to thank our family and friends who always lightened the load through their support and love. Jason Silverman wishes to thank his wife Susan and their son, Alex, without whom it would all be meaningless. All good things in his life begin and end with them and the love and joy they bring to his life is, without doubt, sustaining. Simple things, like playing with Alex or going for a walk with Susan, are truly the important and priceless things in his life. Perhaps this book and the others could have been completed quicker by sequestering himself away in the study, but in the process too much would have been missed and the cost would have been too high. He will always remember the picture-perfect November day they all went searching for Tabernacle Cemetery, between Greenwood and Cokesbury, South Carolina, to find the final resting place of Shanks Evans and his family. Hiking through the fall leaves in a remote wooded area not easily found on any map, the Silvermans came across a small hallowed area where, through the vivid fall colors, Shanks's monument became visible. Finding the cemetery was memorable enough; however, the Silvermans also happened upon a proud member of the S.C.V., Rob Allison, and his daughter, who were diligently volunteering their time to clean and restore the monuments and the grounds. There, as the November sun began to wane, they talked about fallen Confederates, Southern heritage and the all but forgotten exploits of men like Shanks Evans and his brother-in-law, Martin Witherspoon Gary, who also lay in Tabernacle Cemetery. We talked about the need to remember the past, learn from it, and never run from it, and the conversation, in that setting and on that day, was truly poignant.

Silverman also wishes to thank his dear friends Tom Appleton, Bob Gorman, and Paul DuBois for greatly enriching his life. The weekly Sunday telephone conversations with Tom, the twice weekly racquetball games with Bob, and the ongoing "cosmic" conversations with Paul all consistently make life enjoyable and exciting. Tom, in particular, turned his legendary editorial skills upon this manuscript and the book is so much the better for it; the authors, as well as Shanks himself, are very fortunate to have prevailed upon Tom's kindness. Tom, Paul, and Bob all personify what it means to be gentlemen and scholars and Silverman's dedication of this book to them, and yet again to Susan and Alex, is but small payment for the happiness that the five of them bring to him. They remind him on a daily basis what truly is important in life and, for that, he is eternally grateful.

Ronald Reagan once said that he put away all of his mother-in-law jokes once he met his wife's mother. The same could be said about Eloise Riel, Jason Silverman's mother-in-law. The personification of a true Southern lady, Eloise, and her late husband, Jim, have always supported all of Silverman's endeavors enthusiastically and proudly. For that, and for far too many other reasons to list, Silverman delights in affectionately acknowledging Eloise's generosity and grace. She is truly all that is good about the South.

Sam Thomas wishes to thank his family for making his work on *Shanks* much easier than it would have been without their love. To Gigi, Steve, Jim, Betsy, Beth, Bailey, Susan, Dawn, and Janet he expresses his deep appreciation for their unwavering and much appreciated support. To Jim and Estelle, he acknowledges that their love and comfort are felt everyday.

Thomas thanks his parents, Sam and Fran, who made him what he is today. Their love and care, their sense of humor, their willingness to question and be questioned, and their ability to pass that on to their children and to their children's children, have all made Thomas a better man. He only hopes that one day he, too, will possess just a fraction of those qualities that his parents possess.

For Thomas, pride in his heritage and in his family gives him a sustaining feeling. As he enters the twenty-first century, it is Thomas's desire to see that his family's pride be passed on to a new generation. Perhaps there will even be a heritage seeker among the next generation of his family. Maggie, Rollie, Maria, Ian, Hanna, Ada, Jacob, Scott, Stephanie, Samantha, Drew, Thomas, and Eliza are all beginning a new chapter of his family's history. To them may it be as exciting as the previous chapters.

Most of all, Thomas again thanks his wife, Lynn, for her support and understanding in this project. It is not easy to juggle numerous projects as we both continue to do without assistance from our spouses.

Thomas also wishes to thank his friends Ed, Margaret, Jai, Van, and Jeannie for helping him with this work more than they will ever know. Without them, he believes, he would have a very boring life and their friendship keeps him grounded in an uncertain and sometimes turbulent world.

Thanks must also be given to Carol Hanlon, History Department secretary at Winthrop University. With uncommonly good cheer, Carol spent more time on this manuscript than either she or Jason Silverman would like to admit and, in the process, learned more about Shanks than she ever desired. But perhaps even more importantly, while handling all of the department's business, she successfully juggled all of Silverman's myriad responsibilities and commitments without ever failing or faltering once and, for that, he truly is appreciative. She is, without doubt, as he has always said, indispensable.

Finally, we would like to express our sincere thanks to our editor, Bob Pigeon. Bob stepped in at a critical juncture in this project and successfully steered it to completion amidst all of the company mergers. Moreover, Bob's word was as good as gold. He did *what* he said he was going to do *when* he said he was going to do it which made working with him a true pleasure. We are grateful for his efforts on our behalf and *Shanks* is so much the better.

Jason H. Silverman
Samuel N. Thomas Jr.
Rock Hill, SC
Spring, 2001

CHRONOLOGICAL TABLE
THE LIFE OF
GENERAL NATHAN GEORGE EVANS

Born, February 3, 1824.

Graduated from West Point, July 1, 1848.

Battle of Wichita, October 1, 1858.

Married Ann Victoria Gary, March 20, 1860.

Resigned from United States Army, February 1861.

Adjutant-General of Regular South Carolina Troops, March 1861.

Bull Run, July 21, 1861.

Leesburg, October 21, 1861.

Promoted to brigadier-general, October 21, 1861.

Voted thanks of Confederate Congress and Mississippi Legislature and medal by South Carolina, 1861.

South Carolina, December 1861, to July 21, 1862.

Second Bull Run and Antietam, July to September 1862.

Kinston Campaign, December 11–17, 1862.

Goldsboro court-martial, February 1863.

Vicksburg, June–July 1863.

Charleston court-martial, October 1863.

Severely injured, April 16, 1864.

Accompanied Davis, April–May 1865.

Engaged in cotton business, 1866.

Midway, Alabama, 1867–1868.

Died, November 28, 1868.

General Nathan George "Shanks" Evans, C.S.A.

INTRODUCTION

History has not been kind to Nathan George Evans, the Confederate general nicknamed "Shanks" as a youth because of his spindly legs. Portrayed as a dark, brooding, self-absorbed figure whose military career plummeted during the Civil War perhaps due to alcoholism or insubordination, Evans has truly never had his day in historical court. Since his death in 1868 at the age of forty-four, the historical record, for the most part, has relied upon what others have said about the general and his behavior. Virtually all biographical sketches of Evans touch on the salient events of his life only to conclude that primary material on the general is sketchy at best, nonexistent at worst.

However, a rather different picture of General Evans emerges when he is allowed to speak for himself. Certainly the Shanks Evans that appears is not the overwhelmingly vain, arrogant, alcoholic, and defiant figure that has plagued his legacy. Quite the contrary, in fact. The Evans who emerges is a devoted family man concerned, in his correspondence, with the well-being of his wife, children, brothers, and other family members. He is a fighting general who frets over the welfare of his troops and who, for the most part, has their respect and affection in return. He is also a general who corresponded with, and offered sought-after advice to, the Confederate high command. While Shanks Evans is assuredly no saint, nor does this book seek to elevate him to that status, so, too, is he not the sinner that history records.

Yet this picture of Nathan Evans is admittedly and decidedly at odds with what others have written. We first encountered the general in our *"Rising Star of Promise": The Civil War Odyssey of David Jackson Logan* (Savas Publishing Co., 1998). Logan was part of South Carolina's storied yet truly neglected "Tramp Brigade," so named because unlike most other Civil War regiments they traveled extensively and fought in whatever theater of war they were needed. We immediately became intrigued with Nathan Evans, the commander of the "Tramp Brigade" and a Confederate general about whom so little had been written. Indeed, what fragments had been written about Evans were, without doubt, overwhelmingly critical and condemnatory. We wondered how a general whose career had been so bright and filled with promise at the outset of the war could be so quickly relegated to the historical backbench without ever hearing much, if anything, from Evans himself.

Thus, we set out to rediscover and recreate the general's life as we had done with the story of David Logan. Finding all of Logan's papers and putting them together was much like hitting the historical lottery, so we doubted that lightning would strike again with the story of Nathan Evans. But evidently lightning sometimes does strike twice in the same place. Persistent and tenacious historical detective work eventually led us to Evans's descendants where we discovered the Shanks Evans mother lode, of sorts—a cache of the general's papers and letters (both to and from) which, quite literally, had never seen the historical light of day. The Evans family, and in particular Gary Evans, whose late father joins us in authorship of this book, generously made available to us Shanks's papers and many of the photographs included herein and published for the first time. This, then, is the first biographical study of Evans undertaken. In ploughing hitherto virgin land we realize the pitfalls and pratfalls inherent in such an endeavor. Not everyone will agree with our approach or the tenor of our work, particularly those predisposed to premature conclusions about Evans; yet, for us, the key to this project is to know what we have written and why we have written it.

Thus, this is a traditional narrative biography of General Nathan George "Shanks" Evans, and we make no apologies for it. We have neither sought to psychoanalyze the general nor vivisect his youth or relationship to his parents and siblings. We have not attempted to write a collective socio-biographical history of the Confederate leadership with Evans at the center nor any other broad-based, all encompassing study. Instead, we have written about Shanks Evans and his personal and military wars. And, in so doing, we hope simply to have presented a different side of the general for the historical record. We have allowed Shanks to speak for himself throughout and present his own case on many of the controversial events in his short life. While we do not wish to deify him, neither do we wish to see him remain silent or permit his adversaries (and there were many) to dominate the conversation.

Beginning with the story of David Jackson Logan in *A Rising Star*, the current biographical study of Nathan Evans represents the second volume in what will be a projected three-volume study of the people and history of the Tramp Brigade. With studies of Logan, a very "uncommon" common soldier of the brigade, and Evans, their commanding officer, now in place, we will conclude our trilogy with a history of the Tramp Brigade itself.

Although he might not agree with all that we say, having studied Shanks Evans, we are relatively confident that he would be pleased to finally have his say. Always colorful and controversial, Shanks Evans and the men around him did yeoman service for the Confederacy. His, and their, story is a good one, and one well worthy of being told.

— Chapter I —

BACKGROUND AND EARLY LIFE

In distant Wales a group of Baptists from the counties of Pembroke and Caermarthen decided to immigrate to America. Because one of their number, Thomas Griffin, was a minister, it was suggested that they be constituted as a church, and the immigrants followed the advice. This body, consisting of sixteen persons, embarked from Willford in June 1701 and landed in Philadelphia on September 8. Their fellow Baptists in that city greeted them warmly and advised them to settle near Pennepek.[1] Two years later, however, because of religious differences, they found it inconvenient to stay at Pennepek.[2] At this time they secured land from Messrs. Evans, Davis, and Willis, who previously had purchased a tract containing about thirty thousand acres from William Penn. The tract was situated in the county of Newcastle in what is now Delaware, about forty-three miles southwest of Philadelphia.

One of the first things the settlers did was to build a meeting house. As the years passed, the church's membership was increased, especially by new arrivals from Wales in 1710, among whom was Thomas Evans from Rhydwilim, Wales. His brother, John Evans, was added to the church by baptism in 1711.[3]

Thomas and John Evans were of the class called "gentlemen," and it is believed that they were descended from the ancient family of Evans that originated in Flint and later branched out into Pembrokeshire and Caermarthenshire. This ancient family descended from the renowned Welsh prince Ethelstan Glodrydd, Prince of Furlys. The arms borne by the family of Thomas and John Evans are the same as those borne by the descendents of the family of Caermarthenshire and Pembrokeshire.

John Evans died in Pencader Hundred in 1717, leaving a will which is recorded in Newcastle County, Delaware. He named his brother, Thomas, as his executor and in the document mentioned four sons, of whom Nathaniel Evans was one.[4]

Thomas and Nathaniel Evans remained in Delaware until 1736, when they decided to emigrate with other members of their church to South Carolina.[5] There the Council at Charles Town had offered to set aside a large tract of land for the sole benefit of the Welsh, and the Evanses decided to avail themselves of this opportunity. This tract of land, containing one hundred and seventy-three thousand acres, was situated in Craven County with the greater portion of the land on the south side of the Great Pee Dee River. The Welsh, however, desired a more extensive grant, so the Council made further inducements. They extended the November 16, 1736, grant by giving the Welsh exclusive rights to all lands eight miles on each side of the Great Pee Dee River up to its main branches.[6] This river, which rises in North Carolina, is noted for its meandering, forming many peninsulas before emptying into the Atlantic Ocean below Georgetown, South Carolina.

This extension of the grant up the Great Pee Dee entitled the Welsh to settle in an extensive territory that embraced more than a hundred miles of the course of the river, its alluvial bottom, and valuable lands near the swamps.[7] The Welsh were quick to take advantage of such wonderful inducements. Among these was Nathaniel Evans. Having been dismissed by letter from the church in Delaware, in November 1736 he was recommended to the church in Charles Town, South Carolina.[8] Nathaniel settled in the lower part of the Welsh Tract on Catfish Creek, one of the tributaries of the Great Pee Dee. He received grants of land near Tart's

Mill, which is approximately six miles from Marion Court House.[9]

After making his holdings secure on Catfish Creek, Nathaniel took up more extensive grants near what is now Marion, South Carolina. Soon he and his kinsmen experienced considerable annoyance and much delay in obtaining their grants, although they had come to Carolina at the invitation of the Council.[10] Because the journey to Carolina had been very expensive, the Welsh had comparatively little, if any, capital when they reached the Great Pee Dee. Indeed, they could not pay to have their lands surveyed. Their plight became so grave in 1742, that Nathaniel Evans and more than a score of other Welsh settlers addressed a petition to the Council requesting that the Council grant them land free from the charges of surveying and granting. The lieutenant-governor in Council responded to this petition by refusing to pay for the surveying but extended the time of the grant by two years. The Council, however, offered a bounty of five pounds currency per barrel on the first twenty barrels of flour shipped to Charles Town from the Welsh settlement, if the Welsh could prove that it came from the Welsh tract.[11]

Whether Nathaniel Evans took advantage of the Council's offer is not known, but it is evident that he soon became fairly prosperous. Patents dating from 1746 to 1772 show that he amassed eleven hundred acres of as fertile land as was to be found in the Welsh grant.[12]

The last extant reference to Nathaniel Evans was a "Memorial" that he presented to the governor and His Majesty's Council on February 12, 1772. It is believed that he died prior to the outbreak of the American Revolution. His age at the time of his death is not definite, but Nathaniel certainly was well advanced in years, as he was born in Wales and arrived at Pencader prior to 1711.

There is some doubt as to the date of his marriage to Ruth Jones,[13] but it is probable that Nathaniel married her after his arrival in South Carolina, because his eldest son, David, was still living as late as 1825. Together, Ruth and Nathaniel had four children: David, Margaret, Thomas and Nathan. Nathan, the youngest, was born around 1760.[14]

The country in which these children were reared was practically a wilderness, and the inhabitants were constantly in danger of attacks from Indians. To offset this hazard, the Welsh settled close together and at first took up only enough land to meet their immediate needs. In their wilderness homes the Welsh were drawn closer together by common ties of blood and friendship. One local observer wrote that "simplicity of character appears to have been one of the most marked traits of this people—a virtue which has been transmitted, through succeeding times, to their descendants." "Open and sincere" they were further distinguished by their "sobriety and moderation."[15]

Though the Welsh had little hard currency on which to live, nature was kind to them; rich pasturage, fertile land, and luxuriant forests abounded. These provided for their necessities; and to add to their good fortune, there was the Great Pee Dee River which offered an easy outlet for their surplus commodities. They quickly cleared the land, developed communication with each other, and secured outlets for trade. Already the Council had offered premiums and other incentives for the cultivation of certain crops.

One of their earliest and most lucrative sources of revenue came from cattle raising and livestock. The Welsh immediately turned their attention to the large numbers of wild horses and cattle abounding in the forest. The horses were captured and domesticated, and stock raising became quite lucrative. Fine pasturage being inexhaustible, the dwindling of the supply of one pasture only necessitated the moving of the cattle to another. The stock was driven to Charles Town and other coastal settlements for sale. Some of the cattle raisers had their stock moved as far north as Philadelphia. Another endeavor which brought revenue was the raising of hogs. Pork soon became one of the leading exports, and "Cheraw Bacon" achieved fame in distant parts of the country. As sawmills were erected soon after the settlers arrived and timber was abundant, lumber was also an important means of revenue. Because neither soil nor climate was suited to hemp and flax, those crops did not prove as profitable as the Welsh had anticipated; so they soon turned to wheat and corn, which proved more lucrative. In the 1740s, it was discovered that the soil along the Great Pee Dee was admirably suited for the growth of the indigo plant. A number of the Welsh enjoyed the cultivation of indigo, which soon became the most valuable crop of the settlement.[16]

The Welsh were confronted with the problem of transporting their prospering wares to market. Because their country was in a wilderness condition, their only outlet was the Great Pee Dee River, which was open from Cheraw down.

Since the existing Indian and animal trails did not meet the needs of the growing population, the Commons House of Assembly passed several acts before the Revolution for the construction of proper roads and causeways. David Evans was one of the men appointed in 1768 to direct these improvements. Conditions were improved by the construction of roads and ferries, but the needs of the Welsh were not satisfied.[17]

In spring 1775, the grand jury of the District of the Cheraws presented the following grievances to the Council: the absence of a new jury list, new bridges, the clearing of the Great Pee Dee River of encumbrances, a vagrant act in the Cheraw Province, and the little notice taken of previous presentments of the grand jury. An "enormous grievance" was also presented by the grand jury, but it was quashed by the judge.[18] The Cheraws's grand jury stated that the American people could not be taxed without their consent and could not be deprived of the right of a trial by jury. The grand jury even went further by declaring that they would be willing to defend these inherent rights at the cost of their lives and property.[19] When the final struggle came, therefore, most of the Welsh were ready to risk their all in the fight for independence.

Although still a youth at the outbreak of hostilities, Nathan Evans, youngest son of Nathaniel Evans, shouldered his musket and joined brothers David and Thomas in fighting for the liberty and freedom which his people had loved so well. He served as a private throughout the war under the gallant Francis Marion. David Evans, a captain of Rangers, lost a leg while participating in the 1780 siege of Savannah under General Nathanael Greene.[20]

Returning home after the war, Nathan found his father's estate on Catfish Creek in a deplorable condition. He immediately set out to replenish his shattered fortune. In time, he succeeded in building up his estate. In 1788, he married Edith Godbold, the grand-daughter of John Godbold, one of the earliest settlers on the Great Pee Dee. She was the sister of Lieutenant Stephen Godbold, one of Marion's men, who had served throughout the Revolution. On September 3, 1790, Edith gave birth to a son who was named Thomas. Another child, Asa, arrived shortly but died in infancy. Edith Evans died soon afterward, and Nathan chose for his second wife a Miss Fore. By this marriage were born two daughters, Edith and Zilpha. Nathan's second wife lived only a few years; and faced with the burden of rearing three infant children, he decided to wed for the third time. The lady of his choice was Elizabeth Anne Rogers, a daughter of Captain Lot Rogers, a staunch patriot, who had come to Carolina from Virginia before the war. By this marriage several children were added to the family: William, Nathan, Elizabeth and John Gamewell. Nathan Evans Sr. prospered in worldly affairs and added land to his estate as the years passed. At his death in 1810, he left an estate consisting of three tracts of land totaling 350 acres and two other tracts with the total number of acres not specified in his will. The estate also included four slaves, much personal property, household goods, cows, horses, hogs, and sheep.

Thomas Evans was born in 1790, a time when his section of the state had not yet fully recovered from the effects of the partisan warfare that had been waged for nearly seven years. This section was sparsely settled and nearly as it was when his ancestors arrived. Although the opportunities for an education were rare, he acquired a liberal education by wide and judicious reading. In early life he devoted his time to mercantile pursuits which soon proved highly profitable. Later, however, he turned to planting and was among the first in his community to engage in the extensive planting of cotton.

On April 11, 1816, Thomas Evans married Jane Beverly Daniel, the daughter of George and Martha Daniel of Granville County, North Carolina. The Daniel family had come to Virginia late in the seventeenth century.[21] But one of Jane Beverly's ancestors, John Woodson, had come to Virginia and settled in Pierseys Hundred in 1619.[22]

On January 10, 1817, Jane Beverly Evans gave birth to the first of thirteen children. This son, Chesley Daniel, was to be one of the signers of the South Carolina Ordinance of Secession. On February 3, 1824, another boy was born to Thomas and Jane Beverly Evans. This time they chose the family name of Nathan, and the baby was christened Nathan George.

Thomas Evans entered the political arena in 1816, and was selected as one of the presidential electors for South Carolina, casting his vote for James Monroe. He continued his interest in politics and became an ardent follower of Andrew Jackson. He was one of the South Carolina electors who voted for Jackson in 1828. His loyalty to Jackson was so pronounced that when his sixth child was born January 1, 1828, Thomas Evans named him Andrew Jackson. However, he was to regret his choice.[23]

In 1828, Congress passed a tariff act which earned the sobriquet the "Tariff of Abominations." South Carolinians thought this tariff unjustly discriminated against their state and interests. Public meetings were called and well attended, their chief note being resistance to the tariff laws.

In August 1828, John C. Calhoun anonymously issued from Fort Hill on the Savannah a document to become known as the "South Carolina Exposition" in which he set forth South Carolina's grievances and proposed a remedy. He urged his fellow citizens to ignore northern goods, to trade with their natural customers, the British, and to declare the tariff act "null and void."

The discussion continued for over a year not only in South Carolina but throughout the nation. Then it blazed forth in the United States Senate in the 1829–30 session. A resolution introduced concerning public lands in the West finally matured into the historic Webster-Hayne debate. In his speech Robert Y. Hayne of South Carolina defended nullification in a most convincing manner, only to be met by one of the greatest speeches ever delivered by Daniel Webster, the American Demosthenes. The senator from Massachusetts gave an extensive argument against nullification, defended the constitution and the supreme court, and urged national unity.

The reply of Webster dampened the hopes of some nullifiers in the South, but the hot-blooded South Carolinians continued their stand against the tariff. Their leaders in Washington were gradually drawing away from the Jackson administration. Finally, Jackson and Calhoun split, and Hayne returned to South Carolina, soon to become governor. In a short time, Calhoun resigned as vice-president to take Hayne's place in the Senate. With no remedy in sight from the tariff, South Carolina decided to take matters into its own hands.

Anxious that a step be taken before the new Congress could assemble, Governor James Hamilton summoned a special session of the legislature to meet in Columbia on October 22, 1832, to consider nullification. On October 25, an act was passed calling for a convention to assemble in Columbia on the third Monday in November to discuss nullification. Delegates to the convention were to be elected on the second Monday and Tuesday in November, and each electoral district was to have as many representatives in the convention as its total representation in the legislature. William Evans, Thomas's younger brother, was chosen as a delegate to represent his county, Marion; and, like his family, he was an ardent exponent of nullification.[24] The convention issued a document declaring that the tariff laws were "null and void" and requested the legislature to enact such legislation as was needed to put the ordinance into effect. As soon as the convention adjourned, the legislature met and passed the laws requested. Andrew Jackson replied to South Carolina's ordinance by his nullification proclamation on December 10, 1832. He stated that if the people of South Carolina refused to obey or resisted the laws of the United States, he would resort to force. At this time Thomas Evans was a member of the state senate. His physical features were so much like those of John C. Calhoun that he was often mistaken for the latter. Their political views proved also to be in agreement. Evans became bitter against the president and began to denounce him.[25]

The nullification crisis was averted by the Compromise Tariff Bill passed by Congress in March 1833. On March 15, South Carolina rescinded its ordinance of nullification. Nevertheless, the seeds were sown that were destined to blossom in another generation.

Nathan George was a youth approaching his ninth birthday

during this heated controversy, and perhaps his desire to become a soldier began at this time. Seeing his Uncle William, who was a brigadier-general in the South Carolina militia by appointment from Governor Hayne, in his military uniform no doubt made a deep impression on the mind of the growing boy.

The disastrous panic of 1837 was a severe blow to Thomas Evans, who had invested heavily in cotton. Because of the great depreciation in its value, he suffered an overwhelming financial loss from which he never fully recovered. He continued to serve in the state senate until 1840, when he retired to become Master in Equity of Marion County, a position he held until his death.

Nathan George received his early education along with his brothers at Marion Academy under Jerry Dargan. Later he entered Randolph-Macon College in Virginia, where he graduated before he had attained the age of eighteen. Returning to his South Carolina home, he began pleading with his father to obtain for him an appointment to the United States Military Academy at West Point. Thomas Evans opposed this desire; but the young man, determined to be an officer, was persistent. Finally, in 1844, he received an appointment from Senator John C. Calhoun to the United States Military Academy. Nathan George accepted the appointment, apparently against the wishes of his father. Yet deep down in his heart this old firebrand of the nullification period may not have been too much opposed to it.[26]

— Chapter II —

FRONTIER SERVICE

Nathan George Evans was admitted to the United States Military Academy on July 1, 1844. He gave his legal address as Marion Court House, Marion County, South Carolina. By the end of his first year he stood, in order of general merit, forty-fifth in a class of fifty-seven members.[1]

During his second year at the academy, sadness descended upon his life. His father, Thomas Evans Sr., had contracted a serious case of pleurisy, from the effects of which he never fully recovered. In summer 1845, Thomas decided that a change of climate would be beneficial to his health. So with his son, James, a lad of fourteen, he made a trip to Virginia, staying at some of the famous springs of that state. His condition, however, did not improve, so he departed from Old Point Comfort for his home in Carolina. To lessen the hardships of the long trip home and also to see his wife's family, he decided to stop at her former home, "Tranquility," in Granville County, North Carolina. After arriving at "Tranquility," his health continued to decline, and he passed away on August 9, 1845, and was buried in the old Daniel family cemetery.[2]

The passing of his father was no doubt a severe shock to the young cadet—especially so, since his father left an estate which was heavily in debt. It must have grieved him to have to remain away from home for such a long period when he felt that his assistance was needed in helping his brothers provide for his mother and her infant children. Despite this adversity, he advanced from forty-fifth place to thirty-sixth in a membership of fifty-two.

It must have been about this time that the four oldest Evans sons, Chesley D., Thomas, Nathan George, and Beverly Daniel, made an agreement with their mother concerning the disposition of their father's estate. The four sons agreed to deed their interest in the estate to their mother for the education of the seven younger children. The four older brothers were to go out into the world and make their places. Devoted to their mother and younger brothers and sister, they were always to be at their call when needed. The talented Mrs. Evans assumed the management of the heavily involved estate. By thrift and shrewd management, she not only took care of the large family but sent them to the leading colleges in America for their higher education.[3]

Whether the course of study became more difficult or for other reasons, nine of the members were dropped from Cadet Evans's class during his third year at the academy. His ranking also suffered, for when the classifications were made he stood thirty-eight in a class of forty-three. The depletion continued to be heavy his final year, but when graduation was held July 1, 1848, he was one of the survivors, finishing thirty-sixth in a class of thirty-eight members which had started four years earlier with fifty-seven. On the same day that Evans was graduated he was commissioned brevet second lieutenant in the United States Army and was honored with the distinction of being assigned to the 1st Dragoons.[4]

Among his fellow cadets at the academy were young men who were later to gain great renown on the battlefields of Mexico, on the American frontier, and in the War Between the States. Some of them were: W. H. C. Whiting, Bernard E. Bee, Ambrose P. Hill, Thomas J. Jackson, E. Kirby Smith, C. P. Stone, Thomas G. Rhett, George B. McClellan, John G. Foster, Innis M. Palmer, James B. Fry, John Buford, William N. R. Beall, Fitz-John Porter, David R. Jones, W. M. Gardner, A. E. Burnside, George E. Pickett, James Oakes, Samuel D. Sturgis, Otis H. Tillinghast, Henry Heth, E. D. Blake, A. J. Donalson Jr., and George H. Stewart.[5]

Lieutenant Evans joined the 1st Dragoons at Jefferson Barracks,

Missouri, on November 11, 1848. After a brief stay there, he was transferred to Fort Leavenworth in January 1849, and thus began a six-year period of frontier service west of the Missouri River. In the summer of 1849, Evans participated in an expedition to the Rocky Mountains.[6]

Young Evans found himself stationed at a place with duties confronting him that would have taxed the merit of an officer with many years' experience. Assigned to the frontier, it was the duty of the Dragoons not only to keep order at their respective stations but to patrol the vast expanse of territory between Missouri and the Pacific Ocean, most of which had been recently acquired from Mexico and which was populated by warlike tribes of Indians. The mad rush to the California gold fields augmented the duties of the United States troops on the western frontier. The number of wagon trains making the long trek across the continent increased. Hostile Indians constantly attacked, causing the settlers to make more demands for protection by the scattered troops of the United States Army.[7]

Lieutenant Evans served at Fort Leavenworth as quartermaster and commissary until January 1850, and from that date until April of the same year as post adjutant. While there the young officer met an attractive young lady to whom he seemed quite attached. He made the following entry in his journal on June 15, 1850: "Left the Fort with the Company at 11:00 o'clock to march a mile and return. Men drink—returned took dinner and proceeded to put Company K in Camp having been in camp an hour returned again to take final adieu. Remained until 1 o'clock in Garrison Sweet parting with Miss X the kiss of first love. We camped today on Salt Creek 3 miles from the Fort."[8]

The three-mile march was the beginning of the expedition to the Crossing of the Arkansas, because the next entry in Lieutenant Evans's journal on August 12 revealed that he was leaving the Crossing of the Arkansas "on detached duty, escorting Government supplies under charge of Mr. Aubrey." The party marched three days without meeting anyone except the wagon trains of Messrs. McCarty and White, who were making a return trip from Santa Fe. Late in the evening of the third day, they arrived at *The*

Cache on the Cimarron. "This point," wrote Evans, "is a place where the bluff comes near the stream [and] takes its name from being the place where Mr. Aubrey's goods were concealed last winter and afterwards taken to Santa Fe by Captain Judd." After passing the night at *The Cache*, the party followed the course of the Cimarron, which Evans described as follows: "Were it not for the appearance of the vegetation . . . . a stranger would never suppose there was anything like a stream running on his left as he marched along the road. It appears like the bed of some small stream that had many years ago been turned into another channel, but by digging along the bed of this apparent dry creek water may be found within two feet of the surface."[9]

They continued their march for three days, camping by night at various sites along the Cimarron and on the third day encamped one and one-half miles above the crossing of the Cimarron. About two hours after camp was made, one of Aubrey's men reported a party of Indians with pack mules. "This looked as if a wagon train had fallen victim to an Indian massacre," wrote Evans. Leaving four men under Sergeant Hulstead to guard the camp and wagon train, Evans took the rest of the troops to search for the Indians. The extensive investigation proved unsuccessful.

The party was now beginning to feel some of the discomforts of a prolonged journey through the barren lands of the West. For several days at a time they had had very little water and had suffered from the intense heat. Supplies of grass and wood became scarce and the heat was broken at intervals by cold rains. The combined effect of heat and rain left the animals nearly lifeless, causing several of them to be left behind at various stops.

In an August 21 entry, Evans gives an interesting description of the scenery from "Round Mound." Accompanied by Mr. Aubrey, he attempted to climb the mountain, but wrote, "We were only partially successful [as] our knees refused to perform their usual functions. Nearly exhausted we stopped about halfway up— Commanding positions. Scenery of the distant mountains and immediate surrounding level prairie extremely grand—rugged cliffs breaking abruptly beautiful slopes of the rolling prairie."[10]

At two o'clock the following afternoon the soldiers came to La

Riviere Don Carlos. There they experienced the shock of finding the remains of Mr. White and his party who had been massacred by the Indians. Lieutenant Evans stopped to give burial to the blanched bones of the unfortunate victims. Their bones had been scattered and broken by the wheels of other trains that had passed over them without stopping. "I could not attempt to describe my feelings, in looking around here," Evans wrote, "while at this spot to behold such striking monuments of Government wanton neglect to protect its travelling citizens. Traces of the lamented Mrs. White are still visible[;] pieces of lace, calico & so forth."[11]

Two days later they arrived at "Wagon Mound," a point notorious for being the scene of the recent murder of ten expressmen. Lieutenant Evans, young and impressionable, had been on frontier duty for two years and perhaps had seen remains of other massacres. But these "monuments of Government wanton neglect" no doubt made him feel more keenly his responsibilities and increased his zeal and vigilance in Indian warfare.

After leaving "Wagon Mound," Evans neglected to make additional entries in his journal, so it is not known when he received his promotion to 2nd Lieutenant in the 2nd Dragoons. His commission, which was to date from September 30, 1849, was signed by President Zachary Taylor and Secretary of War George W. Crawford on the 27th day of June 1850. This commission was one of the last signed by President Taylor who died a few days later. On July 8, a letter containing his commission and the following orders was sent by Assistant Adjutant-General Lorenzo Thomas: "You will report, by letter, to the Colonel of your Regiment, and join your Company (E) at Socorro, New Mexico." A month later Evans was at the Crossing of the Arkansas, so it is surmised that he left before receiving orders to report to Fort Socorro. He reported, however, to Fort Socorro in 1850.[12]

Evans gained for himself quite a reputation as an Indian fighter while in New Mexico. In 1851, he was transferred to Fort Conrad, New Mexico, where he participated in several campaigns against the Apache Indians. On one of these campaigns the Apaches were met in battle near the Laguna on the Jornado del Muerto on January 24, 1852. Evans was next sent to Fort Webster, New

Mexico, where he remained until 1853. It was in the West that Evans acquired a devoted servant while on scouting duty. Coming by chance upon a party of hostile Indians and hearing cries of pain, Lieutenant Evans's party went to investigate. They found the Indians torturing a Mexican peasant by shooting arrows at him for the amusement of their women. The Indians were driven off and Evans cut their captive from the tree to which he had been tied. This Mexican, who was afterwards known as Gabriel, refused to leave the side of his rescuer and remained his loyal servant for a number of years. When Evans was transferred to Fort Leavenworth in 1853, Gabriel accompanied him. Except for a visit to his Carolina home, Evans's stay at Fort Leavenworth was uninterrupted until 1855 when he was promoted to first lieutenant in one of the newly formed cavalry regiments.[13]

These cavalry regiments were to assist the overburdened troops on the frontier in protecting the settlers from the depredations of the Indians and renegades. Congress had been asked for a number of years to provide for the sorely needed additional troops. It was through the perseverance of the secretary of war, Jefferson Davis, and the recommendations of President Franklin Pierce that the bill providing for more troops was finally brought before Congress during the 1854–55 session. After a heated debate in Congress that lasted several months, the bill was finally passed on March 2, 1855.

As soon as the legislation was signed, the War Department proceeded to complete the organization of the new regiments. A general order was promulgated to the army on March 26, 1855, which put into operation the provisions of the bill and announced the regimental officers of the 2nd Cavalry. Albert S. Johnston was appointed colonel; Robert E. Lee, lieutenant-colonel; and William J. Hardee and Walter Emory, majors. Nathan George Evans was the senior 1st lieutenant of the regiment. Major Emory was transferred to the 1st Cavalry on May 26, 1855, and Captain George H. Thomas of the 3rd Artillery was selected to fill the vacancy. Other changes were that Kenner Garrard was made adjutant and Richard W. Johnson was appointed quartermaster.[14]

Sectional strife now began to darken the path of Nathan George

Evans. Leaders from both North and South looked upon the new regiment with distrust. Northern critics charged that Davis, a native of Mississippi, had carefully selected officers from the southern states, while the southern firebrands took the view that the new troops were to form the nucleus of an army to coerce the southerners on the states rights issue.

It was unjustly charged that the newly appointed officers were "creatures" of Jefferson Davis, for events were later to prove that these men were "creatures" of no man. Whether their duties called them North or South during the War Between the States, they gallantly distinguished themselves on many battlefields and their names became household words in their respective sections.[15] Indeed, it has been said that the 2nd Cavalry "turned out during the War more distinguished men than any other regiment in the army."[16]

Evans received his promotion to 1st Lieutenant in the 2nd Cavalry while on duty at Fort Leavenworth. Soon afterward he was ordered to report for duty at Louisville, Kentucky, where the 2nd Cavalry was to be organized; he arrived there May 28, 1855. The headquarters of the regiment remained at Louisville until early September when it was transferred to Jefferson Barracks, Missouri.

Lieutenant Evans was assigned to Company F, which was under the command of Captain Theodore O'Hara.[17] Because of the late arrival of some of the officers, the recruiting did not get under way until around the twentieth of May. Officers of the various companies were soon sent to different parts of the nation to fill their companies. Company F was recruited at Louisville by Captain O'Hara.

Evans's stay in Louisville was brief, for he soon departed from there with a detachment of recruits which he conducted to Jefferson Barracks, where they arrived on June 5. There he served under Lieutenant-Colonel Lee and Major Hardee, who were in charge of the conditioning of the recruits at the post.[18] The camp life at Jefferson Barracks was anything but desirable during the summer. A number of the men were sick; and when cholera made its appearance, the men became greatly alarmed. Added to these discomforts, they suffered from lack of sufficient clothing. Requisition for supplies had been made early in May, but because of faulty transportation facilities provisions did not arrive until the latter part of September.[19]

To make matters worse for the young lieutenant, he received a letter from a lady who regretted that he could not attend a party at Fort Leavenworth. She recommended that he take courting lessons from the 1st Cavalry, which had replaced them at Fort Leavenworth. After saying that Flora was very anxious to have him come, she said, "Mr. Stewart [J. E. B. Stuart] is seen before breakfast, and late at night on the piazza— I do not know but he boards there."[20] Although the life in camp was more disagreeable than the enlisted men had anticipated, it did not hinder greatly their willingness to learn the arts of frontier warfare; so the regiment was ready for service when the orders to march to the frontier were issued. In view of the conditions that had prevailed at the camp during the summer, Lieutenant Evans must have been happy when he was ordered to Detroit, Michigan, to recruit some new men. He remained there until the middle of October, returning to Jefferson Barracks on October 25.

On October 27, the 2nd Cavalry began its long trek to western Texas. The regiment marched from Jefferson Barracks in a southwesterly direction over the Ozark Mountains and followed generally the line of the Pacific Railway surveys. The cavalry passed through Waynesville and Springfield and then along the Missouri boundary line to Maysville, Arkansas, and southwest from there into the Indian territory. Before the cavalry had reached Arkansas, the quartermaster, R. W. Johnson, was taken sick and had to retire to his ambulance. He asked that Lieutenant Evans be detailed to assist him with his duties, and it was so ordered. Johnson turned over the keys to the safe to Evans, who disbursed the money and took full charge of Johnson's duties until his recovery some time later. Johnson praised Evans in no uncertain terms: "I found that Evans had been remarkable careful in his disbursements, as I knew he would be, and my cash balanced to a cent, while all the property which I was responsible was duly accounted for. I knew Evans well, and was never associated with a more honorable, companionable gentleman."[21]

The cavalry arrived at Tahlequah, the capital of the Cherokee Nation, on November 27, and were surprised to find the Indians well advanced in civilization, with brick houses and a fine seminary. When they crossed the Neosho and Arkansas Rivers and entered into Creek territory, a driving "norther" caught them, adding greatly to the discomforts of the march, but the regiment continued to advance. After crossing the North Fork of the Canadian River on December 4, the men soon came to Mica, an Indian village where a large delegation of Seminoles had assembled to trade and visit. The regiment encamped nearby and the next day forded the Canadian River.

Continuing their march, the 2nd Cavalry encamped on December 7 near a large village of Choctaws, and five days later arrived at Fort Washita where a general court-martial was in session that had brought a number of officers to the post. Upon the arrival of the 2nd Cavalry, a salute was fired by Captain Braxton Bragg's battery, and the travel-worn officers were accorded a treat when the hospitable butler, Sam Humes, gave a dinner in their honor.[22]

There were at least fifty officers to partake of Humes's hospitality, for he had invited the officers of the post, which included those attending the court-martial. When cavalry men gathered, discussion over the speed of horses was inevitable. Evans had a thoroughbred Glencoe colt purchased in Kentucky, of which he was very proud. He often boasted that his horse, Bumble-Bee, could outrun any horse in the regiment. While at the dinner, he offered to race his favorite against any horse at Fort Washita. This appeared to be a safe proposal because most of the horses at the fort belonged to a light battery and were more suited for draft than for the turf. Nevertheless, Lieutenant Oliver D. Greene accepted the proposal and selected an artillery horse. According to the agreement, Evans and Greene were to ride their respective mounts. When the starting signal was given, Bumble-Bee dashed away and won, as was expected.[23]

After enjoying the hospitality of the fort for a day or so, the regiment departed and crossed the Red River on December 15 proceeding thence to Preston, Texas. They came to Upper Cross Timbers on the nineteenth, a place to be impressed in their memories by the suffering of the horses from scarcity of water. On December 22, when near their journey's end, about sixty miles northeast of Fort Belknap, the regiment encountered a severe "norther." This delayed them a few days, but they plodded on in weather below zero and arrived at Fort Belknap on December 27.

The territory assigned to the 2nd Cavalry extended from the Rio Grande on the south to the Arkansas River on the north and from the Indian Territory boundary to New Mexico. The chief inhabitants of this vast region were the Lipan, Kiowa, Apache, and Comanche Indians, but the Comanches were regarded as the rulers of this domain. For years it had been their custom to raid the inhabitants of the northern Mexican states and Texas. Sometimes their raids even carried them into Louisiana and Arkansas. The frontiersmen often pursued them, but the Indians invariably escaped to their hide-outs with considerable booty because they were mounted on fast, agile ponies that easily eluded their pursuers.

With the acquisition of the territory from Mexico, the United States had attempted to stop these raids, but the chain of forts that had been established along the frontier and in the Indian Territory was so poorly garrisoned that they could not halt the Indians, and the raids continued. At the time of the arrival of the 2nd Cavalry the Indians had been particularly active. It appeared that the 2nd Cavalry had some exciting and arduous service ahead.

Lieutenant Evans and other members of the 2nd Cavalry were now entering upon an assignment that was to keep them busily engaged until the outbreak of civil war in 1861. During the next few years, because of the 2nd's successful campaigns against the Indians, the settlers on the Texas frontier lived in comparative safety. The life of this brave band of soldiers was a happy one, considering the dangers and hardships encountered. It was as variable and changeable as the days on the frontier were long. To be successful against the Indians the soldier had to rely upon his individuality. After he had seen service for several years on the frontier, he became suspicious of its dangers and was always looking for them. The seasoned veteran was so accustomed to this that watchfulness became a part of his life. This trait clearly marked the difference between an experienced soldier or frontiersman and a raw recruit who, being unaccustomed to vigilance, often paid the penalty by forfeiting his life.

When the regiment arrived at Fort Belknap, orders were received assigning companies B, C, D, G, H, and I to the old post at Fort Mason on the Rio Llano, while the remaining four companies A, E, F, and K, under Major Hardee's command, were ordered to establish a post near the Indian Reservation on the Clear Fork of the Brazos. This station was about forty miles from Fort Belknap, and it was the duty of the men there to watch the activities of the northern and middle Comanches. Major Hardee arrived on January 3, 1856, and chose a spot a mile above the Reservation for the post. The station was named Camp Cooper, in honor of Samuel Cooper, the adjutant-general of the Army. Lieutenant Evans arrived on the same day as Hardee and was to remain there for two years. Evans was well trained for the arduous duties expected of him for he had spent almost all of his time since graduation from military academy upon the frontier. In the next few years he was to experience many thrills as well as innumerable dangers, but this was the life that the Welshman loved.

Now that the companies had arrived at a permanent post, it would seem that the life in camp would improve their living conditions, but such was not to be the case. The companies spent the winter in tents, and it was their bad fortune to endure one of the worst winters in the history of that locality. Having experienced the effects of one "norther" in their march to Texas, they must have been somewhat downhearted after reaching Camp Cooper to experience one after another during the remainder of the winter. The horses suffered severely since there were no stables for them, and often they would be found covered with sleet. An attempt was made to build a shelter for them but vainly, because of the poor material which was at the disposal of the men. To make the best of a bad situation, two companies formed their picket lines under the shelter of the high banks of a nearby creek, while the others formed theirs along the mountain side. Although the horses survived this severe weather, they died in large numbers when fair weather came because of the staggers, which was prevalent to an alarming extent. There was a bright side, however, to this bad situation. Hunting was excellent near the camp, and the men took full advantage of this, not only to relieve the monotony of camp life but to educate themselves in riding and shooting as well as to gain an accurate knowledge of the surrounding terrain.[24]

In the early summer of 1856, the command of the Department of Texas was given to Colonel Johnston, who continued also to command the regiment with his headquarters at San Antonio. Not long after his arrival in Texas in March 1856, Lieutenant-Colonel Robert E. Lee was assigned to the command of the troops stationed at Camp Cooper, and he relieved Major Hardee on April 9, 1856.[25]

On May 1, Captain Charles E. Travis was dismissed from the army, and since Evans was the senior lieutenant in the regiment, he was promoted to fill the vacancy.[26] He remained stationed, however, at Camp Cooper. That same year one of his younger brothers, William Edwin Evans, was graduated from the United States Naval Academy at Annapolis.[27]

The Comanches had been restless again, and Lieutenant-Colonel Lee was placed in command of an expedition composed of companies A and F from Camp Cooper and B and G from Fort Mason to march against them.[28] The command left Fort Chadbourne on June 18, and proceeded to the headquarters of the Brazos and Colorado Rivers, where Captain Earl Van Dorn succeeded in overtaking a body of Comanches and successfully routed them.[29] Lee returned to Camp Cooper on July 23. The detachments of his command had covered some sixteen hundred miles with little to show for their efforts.

While on the expedition, Lieutenant-Colonel Lee assigned Captain Evans to reconnoiter the territory in the vicinity of the headwaters of the Brazos and Colorado Rivers and to report whether a site could be found that would be suitable for a summer encampment. Captain Evans proceeded as directed and upon his return reported verbally that he had found a place which was suitable, being well supplied with wood, grass, and water. One observer noted that:

Lieutenant-Colonel Lee quietly listened until the Captain had completed his verbal report, and then, with a merry twinkle in his eyes, said: 'Captain, your report is quite satisfactory; but did you drink of the water to ascertain if it was good?' Captain Evans instantly replied: 'By Jove! I never thought to taste the water.' Those who remember 'Shanks Evans' will appreciate the quiet joke at his expense.[30]

The nickname of "Shanks," which Evans acquired while at West Point because of the thinness of his legs, was to follow him throughout his career.[31]

After spending many tiresome days upon the plains, the regiment had a respite during the summer at an event that has been termed the "Fort Mason Derby." The main attraction at the "Derby" was a race between Captain Evans's famous Bumble-Bee and Lieutenant Walter Jenifer's Gray-Eagle, both fine thoroughbred horses descending from imported sires. Bumble-Bee was a thoroughbred colt of imported Glencoe, while Gray-Eagle was from Wilton Brown, a colt of imported Priam.

Because of a court-martial being held at the fort, there were a number of officers in attendance, including Colonel Albert Sidney Johnston and Major George H. Thomas. The race created a great deal of excitement, officers betting baskets of champagne and even pay checks, while the ladies wagered gloves and handkerchiefs. The betting was even, but Gray-Eagle was the favorite of the ladies because of his elastic step and beautifully combed mane and hair.

Lieutenant Cornelius Van Camp, considered to have few peers in close-seat riding in the regiment, was astride Bumble-Bee, while Lieutenant Jenifer, an experienced rider in gentlemen races in civil life, was mounted on Gray-Eagle. When the signal to start was given, Van Camp dashed for the inside but Gray-Eagle did not move. Jenifer claimed a false start, which Van Camp acknowledged. He started to return, but Evans yelled "go on." Bumble-Bee ran the heat without competition as Gray-Eagle remained at the starting post. The judges allowed the heat after a lengthy debate, and Evans claimed the race, but since no distance had been agreed upon another heat was ordered. This time the heat was run and Bumble-Bee emerged the winner by a short length in a closely contested race. The race was thoroughly enjoyed by the ladies, who waved their handkerchiefs, and by the officers and men, who yelled themselves hoarse. Captain Albert G. Brackett, with his usual dry wit, gave as his reason for Gray-Eagle's defeat that the horse's black hair was too nicely adjusted.[32]

In fall 1856, Evans was back at Camp Cooper and in receipt of two very interesting letters from Lieutenant-Colonel Lee, who was attending a court-martial at Fort Brown. Lee related the army news and lamented the fact that the court-martial was progressing so slowly. After reading the very vivid description that Lee gave of the celebration at Matamoros, Evans must have wanted to leave the frontier and partake of the gaieties at that place.[33]

With the experience acquired the previous year, the 2nd Cavalry was better prepared to cope with the Indians. Several expeditions were made against them by the various companies, at times divided into smaller detachments. They met with varied success. The Indians by early summer, after several defeats, retreated to their hide-outs in the hills and left the settlements comparatively quiet.

A change was made in the command of the Department of Texas on May 18, 1857, when Brigadier-General David E. Twiggs relieved Colonel Johnston of the command. Johnston was instructed to proceed to Washington, where he received orders to lead the Utah expedition. Lee succeeded Johnston in command of the 2nd Cavalry. Johnston never again served with the 2nd Cavalry, but his brilliant career was watched with soldierly pride by both officers and men of his former command.

In August, Evans received another letter from Lee which told of the different developments in the Texas Department and also brought news of great importance to the militant Welshman. Lee told of the possibility that the 2nd Cavalry might be called to follow Johnston to Utah. Welcoming a chance to fight as much as his liberty-loving ancestors, Evans must have been overjoyed at the possibility. Lee's letter in part read,

> I requested the captain to send you a keg of old whisky I had secreted. I have intended to bring it out some day, & surprise you with it, when yours was exhausted, but now you must take it as

it is. It is counterpart of that I carried up last spring for you. I have never opened it, & thereby have lost my *water* keg, in which it is contained. Save the keg for me don't let Queens or Sublette, and that Set drink up the good liquor—You see there are to be great changes at Camp Cooper, and our Infry. Friends are to be taken from us – I am sorry they are to go so far, but it may be a better place than where they are.

There is no news here. Col. Johnston it is supposed is to go to Utah. Genl Harney to remain in Kansas – So probably in the Spring we may be all trotting out there after him . . . .[34]

Lee wrote to Evans again on August 25, in answer to his request for a leave of absence.

I have recd. your kind letter of the 14th & am very much obliged to you for your attention to my mare-

I have presented your application for a leave of absence to the A. Adjt. Gent- & told General Twiggs how the officers & men were situated at Camp Cooper & that they really had a hard time of it. At present there were but three officers there, & that from the length of time you had been on the frontier, you really were entitled to the indulgences, but that under the circumstances as you were too good a Soldier to expect me to recommend it *now*, & that I hoped that he could make some arrangements to justify it. He said that he had refused Capt Caldwells application, & Capt Stonemans on the same principle & that he could not grant yours – I am very sorry that the circumstances are such as to prevent my recommending your leave as you desired, but should they give us any brevets, or should McArthur or Eagle return to duty I will urge the Genl. to grant either Stonemans or your application. I cannot urge both, and Stonemans has the advantage of precedence –

Your Godfather [Twiggs] says he wants to see you–He is very Well and rides out every day.[35]

Captain Evans received another letter from Lee, dated August 28, from San Antonio, telling of sending up Evans's slave who was given to him by his mother, Jane Beverly Evans:

I send up by train today your woman. It had been the intention of the Qr. Mr. to send up the saddles by the contractors train, which would have given her a long pilgrimage equal to that of the Israelites of old. I discovered it and got it changed. I have selected a wagon for her, & asked Capt. McLean to give the Wagon Mr. special instructions about her- That she is to be allowed to sleep in the wagon etc, & the recruits that go to Colorado are to be confined to the *other* wagons. She has her provisions, bedding & baggage- She says she will pay her way up & I hope she will reach you safely & comfortably. She appears to be a very good woman, & I hope you will have great comfort in her.

P.S. I have written to Major Thomas to ask him to see that your woman has all she wants.[36]

A letter from Lee dated September 15, 1857, brought interesting news to Evans, who was still on the frontier:

The mare arrived safe & sound last Saturday, (12). I am very much obliged to you for the good care you took of her & your directions concerning her. Dillsworth Shoes stood well but the most remarkable among the arrivals is my *water keg*. I never expected to see it again, & in truth extended my claim to it, more to keep me in your mind, to make you feel you had something to do for me, than under the expectation of ever realizing from it a drink of cool water. If it would have been of any use to you, I would rather you had retained it, though the body without the spirit is a lifeless concern.

In reply to your question as to the return of Col. Johnston, I send you the enclosed telegraphic despatch, which seems to be the most authentic account we have reced. I have heard that Genl. Harney had been detained in Kansas at the special request of Govr. Walker, but why Col Sumner with his Regt. Was not sent to Utah, & Col. Cook retained in Kansas with the 2nd Dragoons, I do not know. The selection I think is complimentary to Col J – & may give us the opportunity of visiting the Saints –

Your old Godfather has gone to Washington – He seems to be very frail. I hope a change of climate may benefit him. He seemed very glad to relinquish his Post.[37]

In the meantime, Captain Evans had departed with his company from Camp Cooper. At the headwaters of the Brazos on September 24, he encountered a party of hostile Indians. The Indians were decisively defeated, losing their horses and baggage and leaving two of their number dead upon the field. After the skirmish, Evans returned to Camp Cooper where he remained stationed for the rest of the year.

As the fall passed and the first of the new year arrived, exciting rumors continued to be circulated in Texas. It appeared that the 2nd Cavalry would be called, as Lee had predicted, to join the Utah expedition. Finally the orders were issued, and the companies of the 2nd Cavalry were directed to concentrate at Fort Belknap. But by the time the troops were ready to depart, the seriousness of the Utah situation diminished and the troops were sent back to their posts in Texas.[38]

At this time General Twiggs recommended a change in the policy of warfare against the Indians. He suggested that the troops should take the offensive instead of the defensive as had previously been their policy. In his opinion, if enough expeditions were kept in the field to keep the Indians at home protecting their families and property, they would be too busily engaged there to commit depredations upon the settlers, and this would convince them that the only way to be safe from attack would be to remain quietly upon their reservations. Pursuing this policy, Twiggs asked for permission to send a force into the Indian Territory that would follow the Comanches to their abodes. While on the expedition, he proposed to have the troops build a wagon road to, or as near to, the Wichita Mountains as possible. In the meantime the Indians were at war. In August, Twiggs was informed that a considerable number of Comanches, Apaches, and Cheyennes were gathering on the Canadian River near the Antelope Hills and had been making raids upon the Choctaw Nation for the purpose of securing enough ponies for excursions into Texas. Matters now became serious. Every indication pointed to a general war with the Comanches and such other Indian tribes as they could induce to join them. The Comanches were committing raids on the Rio Grande, which could be easily forded, and were even stirring up trouble on the Comanche Reservation on the Clear Fork of the Brazos. The disturbing influences among the Indians added to the alarm of both officers and men at Camp Cooper. This situation at the Reservation was enough to create alarm, and the leaders were arrested. The army wanted to keep peace there because the Comanches had been encouraged to settle down, cultivate the soil, and send their children to school.

Following General Twiggs's suggestions, an expedition under the command of Captain Earl Van Dorn composed of Companies A, F, and H, and K, a detachment from the 1st Infantry, and some sixty Delaware and Caddo braves were ordered to proceed from Fort Belknap and to establish a supply station on Otter Creek in the Choctaw Nation. This station was to be garrisoned by the infantry detachment, while it was to be the duty of the cavalry and friendly Indians to reconnoiter the territory between the Red and Canadian Rivers, and between 100 and 104 degrees west longitude. Although the force was not so large as was desired, it was all that could be spared at the time. The expedition, including Evans, left Fort Belknap on September 15, 1858, and arrived eight days later at Otter Creek, where a stockade was built in order to enable the infantry to protect the animals and supplies while the cavalry was away.[39] Van Dorn named the camp "Camp Radziminski" in memory of Charles Radziminski, a former officer of the regiment who had died at Memphis, Tennessee, a month earlier on August 18.[40]

Returning to camp on September 22, the Indian scouts brought information as to the whereabouts of the Comanches encamped near the Wichita village in the Choctaw Nation on Horse Creek.[41] The scouts estimated that the encampment was about forty miles nearly east of the stockade. The cavalry set out that afternoon hoping to reach the Comanche encampment in time for an attack by daybreak the following morning. The Indian scouts, unaccustomed to measuring distance by miles, had greatly underestimated the distance, and instead of the estimated forty miles the journey proved to be around ninety. The cavalry, therefore, proceeded until late the following afternoon when a halt was called to rest the horses and to make coffee. As darkness fell, the march was resumed through rough country with numerous ravines that made the progress slow and tedious.

At daybreak, the party marched rapidly over a rolling prairie with ridges on each side. At this time, the Indian scouts who were in advance sent back word that the hostile encampment was near. Orders were promptly issued, and the command was divided into four columns with instructions to deploy and charge when in sight of the camp. The camp was soon discovered located in a splendid defensive position in a cluster of deep ravines near the Wichita village. The surprise was complete. The camp was quiet and it appeared that most of its inhabitants were asleep. Although the officers and men were nearly exhausted after their long march, they now became exuberant as they sensed the nearness of their adversaries and the excitement of the conflict that was to begin in a few moments. The sharp notes of the bugles sounding the charge broke the stillness of the crisp October morning. This was immediately followed by the cheers of the onrushing cavalry as they galloped 225-strong through the thick undergrowth into the village to engage a thoroughly unsuspecting force of twice their numbers. Taken completely by surprise, many of the Indians hid in the lodges, while others dashed into the conflict as soon as they were aroused, and a few even took time to don their war costumes. The Indians soon recovered from their surprise and put up a strong resistance. For about two hours the fierce and exciting battle raged. The once-peaceful morning was now all bedlam as the yells of the soldiers answered the war-whoops of the Indians. Rifles sent their messages of death, arrows flew through the air, sabers flashed as charges and counter-charges were made, and to add to the spectacle, there were many hand-to-hand fights.[42]

Captain Evans was in the thick of the conflict, and while engaged in hand-to-hand combat slew the noted Comanche chief Iruquois. In another hand-to-hand engagement, the brave Carolinian killed an Indian standard bearer with a pistol shot and took possession of the enemy flag. He successfully defended the flag and carried it off the field of battle.[43] The flag, about seven feet long and fastened to a long pole, was made of black-and-white eagle feathers with a strip of red flannel attached. This was one of the first flags known to have been carried by the Indians and was probably an imitation of the United States flag. Evans also captured from the chief his spoon (Comanche chiefs carried spoons), which was made from a buffalo horn.[44] Evans, although busily engaged in battle with his life often at stake, did not overlook the defenseless Indian women and children who were pleading with him for protection. He immediately gave commands to his men that assured their safety.[45] After some two hours of fighting, the Indians were completely routed and fled in all directions. They were pursued by the cavalry for several miles, and numerous warriors were slain outside of the village.

Since the Wichitas were friendly and had been held practically as prisoners in their own village by the Comanches, they were given due consideration. After the battle, a Wichita woman rode up and astonished the soldiers by asking in excellent English to see the commanding officer. When the request was granted, she then stated that the Comanches had seized ponies belonging to her tribe and asked that they be returned. Her entreaty was heard, and it is believed that the Wichitas were able to retrieve all of their stolen horses.

The victory was complete. It was one of the most impressive victories ever achieved over the Comanches, and they never recovered from its effects. The Comanches lost their prestige among the other Indian tribes, and their previous reputation no longer enabled them to persuade other tribes to join them in raids as in the past. The Comanches lost fifty-six braves on the field of battle; many more were killed in the pursuit. Because the Indians carried their wounded from the field, their number is not known, but it is estimated that about one hundred warriors were wounded.[46] The Comanche camp of one hundred and twenty lodges was destroyed and three hundred horses were taken along with arms, ammunition, and numerous supplies. The Indians who escaped to the hills were left in destitute circumstances. Although the cavalry had won the battle, they suffered some casualties. Van Camp, while gallantly charging the enemy, was pierced to the heart with an arrow and instantly killed. Three enlisted men lost their lives and another was fatally wounded. Van Dorn was badly wounded twice, and nine enlisted men received severe wounds.[47] Approximately twenty horses were killed or wounded. It was thought at first that Van Dorn's wound through the body would prove fatal, but he recovered quickly and not only wrote his report of the engagement on October 5, but was back in the saddle in five weeks.

The headquarters of the Department of Texas warmly congratulated the command in general orders "as deserving the highest mead of commendation that could be bestowed, as it had achieved victory more decisive and complete than any ever recorded in the history of Indian warfare." Hearty congratulations were also received from the headquarters of the army and from General Winfield Scott.

Evans was complimented in orders from the army headquarters for conspicuous gallantry, and General Twiggs, who was greatly impressed with the coolness, discretion, and courage which Evans displayed during the battle, recommended him to the War Department for brevet promotion.[48]

The victorious troopers returned to Otter Creek on October 10, and there gained a much-needed rest until October 28 when they again set out in search of the Comanches. This time under the command of Captain Whiting, they scouted the Antelope Hills and the country adjacent to the North and South Canadian Rivers. Their search, however, was fruitless, so they returned around the middle of November without having engaged the enemy.

The citizens of Texas were enthusiastic in their praise of the victorious cavalrymen. The Wichita fight and Van Dorn were the inspiration of both song and stories for many years among the Texans. One of Van Dorn's sisters composed a song which she dedicated to him and called "The Wichita March." The martial tune was played wherever the 2nd Cavalry went in the years that followed.[49]

Upon his return, Evans was assigned to Camp Radziminski, where he remained several months. During this time he participated in additional field service. He was thinking, however, of his Carolina home and of his loved ones whom he had not seen in nearly five years. After waiting for over a year and a half, he obtained a leave of absence on February 15, 1859.[50]

In the latter part of March, Captain Evans arrived in Charleston, where he was received by an enthusiastic populace. The people of his native state were exuberant in their praise of a fellow Carolinian who had so distinguished himself in Texas. The day after his arrival at Charleston, there appeared an article in the Charleston *Courier* under the title "A FURLOUGH WELL EARNED." The *Courier* stated that it was pleased to greet Captain Evans in such good health after his hard campaigns against the Indians on the frontier. It further praised the Captain for the gallant and prominent part he had played in the battle of Wichita. The article ended by declaring that Evans's relatives and friends might well be congratulated on his return in good health on a liberal furlough after a five years' absence spent in service against the Indians.[51]

A short time after his arrival in Marion, Evans showed the Indian flag which he had captured at Wichita to the staff of the Marion *Star*. He consented to leave the flag at their office a few days so that anyone who desired to see it could do so. The *Star* described the flag and also the manner in which Evans had taken it.[52]

The inhabitants of his native district, Marion, greeted him with even more enthusiasm than he had received at Charleston. A meeting of the citizens of the district was held to welcome Captain Evans and to pay respect to his meritorious services in the Comanche campaign. The meeting, acting upon the suggestions of Colonel C. W. Miller, unanimously agreed to call the citizens of Marion District to assemble at Marion on April 5, to pay respect to Captain N. G. Evans.[53]

The public meeting was held in the courtroom at Marion, with Benjamin Gause in the chair and Jno. McLenaghan acting as secretary. Gause stated that the object of the meeting was to prepare "a suitable compliment" to Captain Evans for his outstanding services against the Indians in Texas. A committee was appointed to call upon Evans and invite him to the meeting. While this committee called on Captain Evans, Colonel Miller introduced several resolutions that were unanimously adopted. Those attending praised Evans for his military activities on the frontier and expressed the abiding esteem in which he was held by his fellow citizens, stating they were grateful for the honor which he had bestowed upon the District of Marion. In addition, an appreciation dinner was planned in his honor on May 18, with John McQueen, Representative in Congress, and other notables invited to attend. Captain Evans would be asked to address those assembled at the dinner.

In offering the resolutions, Colonel Miller made a stirring speech praising the position of the soldier who fights for the safety and honor of his country and gives the credit of his deeds to God. Miller continued:

> Of all great actions achieved, let us give God the glory. And now, when we propose to honor our good and true public servant, Capt. N. G. Evans, for his courageous and magnanimous conduct in the Comanche war, we must attribute all the merit of his deeds to the Spirit that rules the destiny of men and nations. We should despise a vicious ambition such as that which made Alexander seek the subjugation of the world, made Caesar cross the Rubicon, made William the Norman slay the English Harold at Hastings, made Bonaparte a villain in distress on St. Helena, and George the Third repentant, at the feet of Washington.
>
> In bestowing a just tribute of respect to our worthy and gallant soldier, Capt. Evans, we will proclaim a refutation of the oft-repeated slander that 'Republics are ungrateful.'
>
> War is justified by Holy Writ. "He that taketh the sword shall perish by the sword." War is the great arm that upholds civil government, which God has ordained for man's happiness. Let us give due praise to him who has done his duty to his country and native District, Marion, in the field of battle against our foes.[54]

Because Captain Evans had not yet been introduced, his brother Thomas, United States district attorney for South Carolina during President Pierce's administration, made suitable response to the preamble and resolutions. Captain A. L. Gregg rose and spoke of the pride that the people of Marion District should feel for having given birth to one who had so distinguished himself fighting for their rights on the distant Mexican frontier. At the conclusion of his remarks, General Wheeler asked for permission to read an extract from the "General Orders," November 10, 1858. He then read an account of the battle of Wichita which described the daring part that Evans played in the engagement.

Those assembled then called for a speech from Colonel W. S. Mullins. The colonel praised the soldier who put true honor ahead of pecuniary fortune and stated that he believed in fostering a military spirit. He concluded his remarks by saying that it would be a pleasure to "commune at the festal board with one who taught us by his example that there was something better than high sounding words and empty declarations."[55]

At this time, Colonel Phillips introduced Captain Evans, noting that he and the captain had been friends since boyhood. He expressed pleasure in having the privilege of introducing one whose accomplishments he so deeply admired. The Marion *Star* recorded Evans's response:

> Capt. Evans said, Gentlemen, *I thank you.* The boon of a soldier is ever to merit the approbation of those who send him. After an absence of five years, I return among you who knew me when I was a boy. During that time, I have been about the business on which you sent me. I have waited anxiously to hear if I had earned your approval. Your 'well-done' of to-day, touches my heart, and stirs my soul with a nobler ambition. He spoke of his native District, of him whose name it bears, placing him high in the roll of military greatness. At a distance it was hard to represent a District which bore his name. That he came from Marion was to him an incentive only less than his sense of duty. Allusion had been made to his conflict with the Indians. He spoke of them historically but briefly, accepted the offer of a dinner, and promised to address the company on that occasion.[56]

The presence of his sister, Sarah Jane, added much to the captain's visit to Marion. Sally, as she was affectionately called by her family and friends, had just completed her studies at the fashionable finishing school for girls that was located at Barhamville near Columbia. At nineteen, she was not only one of the belles of the state, but was accomplished in music and the languages. Since she was the only girl in a large family of boys, she was the center of their attentions.

Soon after her arrival, Captain Evans insisted that she accompany him on a trip through the eastern states as his guest. So Sally, after remaining at home but a short time, accompanied her brother on a trip which included the leading resorts of that day. They visited the Virginia and Saratoga Springs and also West Point. Returning via New York and other large cities of the Atlantic coast, they visited Washington, and while there made a trip to Mount Vernon, where their photographs were made together in front of Washington's tomb.[57] After a trip of several months they arrived home in Marion, where "Sally was the admiration of her friends and the toast of the county."[58]

Evans continued to have honors bestowed upon him. This time it was his native and beloved state of South Carolina which honored him. The House of Representatives and the Senate of South Carolina passed the following resolutions in December 1859:

> Resolved, unanimously, That the General Assembly highly appreciates the gallant and meritorious conduct of Capt. N. G. Evans, of the Second Regiment of the United States Cavalry, in the sanguinary battle of Wichita, fought on 1st October, 1858.
>
> Resolved, unanimously, That his Excellency the Governor be requested to procure a suitable sword, and present the same on behalf of this State, as a testimonial of the estimation in which she holds this distinguished officer.[59]

About this time something was happening even more important to Evans than the honors which were being bestowed upon him. While visiting his aunt, Mrs. Thomas Turpin, near Cokesbury, South Carolina, he became engaged to Anne Victoria Gary,[60] the charming daughter of Dr. Thomas R. and Mary Anne Porter Gary, the latter being a direct descendant of John Knox, the reformer, and King Robert II of Scotland.[61] On March 20, 1860, Miss Gary and Captain Evans were married at Cokesbury. Captain Barnard E. Bee, a fellow student of Evans at West Point, acted as his best man.[62] Shortly thereafter the bride and groom left to begin their new life together in Texas.

Chapter III

SECESSION AND WAR

When they arrived at San Antonio, Texas, in March 1860, Captain Evans and his bride were royally entertained by the officers of the regiments and their friends. Lieutenant Colonel Robert E. Lee and the other officers presented them with a beautiful set of china as a wedding gift.[1]

The young bride, who remained at San Antonio when her husband was sent to Ringold Barracks, vividly described their life in Texas in a letter to her sister, Mrs. Mary Elizabeth Griffin of South Carolina:

> I would have written before this but have been waiting to know what we were going to do. Capt. left this morning with sixty men for Ringold Barracks about two hundred miles from this place. It will take him four weeks to make the trip, so you can imagine how lonely I will be without my Capt. He is the best man in the world your husband not excepted. This is a gay and fashionable place. I have been to two balls since I have been here danced of course. The ladies of the army are all gay and fashionable as nice as you will find anywhere. I dined with Mrs. Duff Monday; had any quantity of wine, all kinds of vegetables. I have returned some of my calls. I never was so tired of receiving calls in all my life. I believe every officer and wife in San Antonio has called besides young officers and ladies. This is headquarters and they are all the time coming and going. Tell Emma she ought to

come here; there are so many nice young officers. I am under Major Grahams and ladys charge. They are nice people. Mrs. Graham is very kind. There are several army ladies boarding here. This is a fine hotel, finer than any in Columbia. Madam Bishop gave a concert here last week. I went and was disappointed in her. I have had several nice rides, also had several carriages offered to me whenever I wish to go out. I have not had my foot on the ground but twice since I have been here. The climate of Texas is delightful . . . . I am busy making up my sheets and pillow cases all linen. I got a nice dinner set and bed room furniture in New Orleans. I am anxious to go to house keeping. Our expenses will be very heavy this year. It cost two hundred dollars to come from home here. Board 2$ a week which we did not expect to do when we came but Capt. could not take me with him he is coming back for me . . . . This is an old and odd looking place; a great many Mexican families. Half the town are Mexican. . . .[2]

In October, Evans was again sent to Camp Cooper. It was about this time that he lost the services of his devoted servant, Gabriel. "Gabs," as he was called by the members of the regiment, became jealous of the attention Captain Evans showered on his young Carolina bride. Thinking that Evans no longer cared for him, he left, heartbroken, and returned to Mexico, never to be heard from again.[3]

Although Evans was on the frontier, his relatives and friends at home kept him well informed of the events that were rapidly pulling the sections of the country apart and that were to change the career of this fiery army officer. In early fall the now-grave condition of the nation took a turn for the worse. Captain Evans was kept apprised of events in his native state by his brother-in-law, Martin Witherspoon Gary, a member of the General Assembly of South Carolina and a fire-eating secessionist:

I have just visited the Executive Chamber, where I had the pleasure of seeing the sword that the State voted to you at the last session. It is one of the most beautiful that I have ever seen. I know you will be proud of it. Tell Vic it made me feel proud that her husband's gallant services had been rewarded in such an appropriate and honorable way.

I write to know if you still desire Gen. S. R. Gist to forward it to you by Adams Express-States and myself have concluded that you had better let it remain here for a time. The state of the Country is too uncertain we think to send it now- but he will await your further order-

The Legislature undoubtedly will call a convention of the people in the event of the election of Lincoln President – And this Legislature is composed of a majority of Separate State action men. I am for a dissolution instanter.

Chestnut – Benham R. B. Rhett – Gov. Adams, & others addressed on last night a large crowd. All the speakers are for secession in the event of the Election of Lincoln –

Minute men are all over the state[;] the Blue cockade is worn by the toddling babe . . . Everything wears the aspect of revolution and war to the knife – There is now a Resolution before the House asking the appropriation of one hundred thousand dollars worth of arms for the State in any emergency. I intend to vote for it.

I hope you will soon have an opportunity of giving the maiden stroke of your beautiful sword in the carcass of some abolitionist. . . .

Even Evans's sister, Sally, after telling of her forthcoming marriage and of her devotion to her brother, brought up the subject of secession:

I'm thinking I will see you & Vic sooner than you expect— that is if you are going to be true to the South for you know there is intense excitement prevailing all over the South – and here in particular, about the last Presidential election. Our State has called a convention on the 17th of December – and it is the universal opinion that she will secede immediately. Florida, Alabama, Georgia, Mississippi, Louisiana and Texas will all follow – and also North Carolina. They are determined to resist Lincoln's election. Everybody is arming, and minute companies are being formed all over the State. Even the ladies are taking part in it by making Flaggs and cockades and waving our handkerchiefs. Every thing is for disunion. Charleston is boiling over with excitement; all business is suspended there. Bro Ches is nominated as a delegate from Marion to the Convention. He is a real hot-headed Secessionist.[4]

These letters from loved ones at home no doubt made a deep impression upon Nathan George Evans, who was on the verge of making the greatest decision of his life. His younger brother, William Edwin, a master in the United States Navy, found himself in the same quandary. Seeking his older brother's advice, he wrote to Captain Evans from Vera Cruz, Mexico.

> You have probably seen in the papers, the great Excitement existing in South Carolina, and the enthusiastic demonstrations for secession – It is pretty generally acknowledged by all that she must and will withdraw from the union in a few days – Now I have been thinking of the matter very seriously and very naturally asked myself the question what I ought to do in that event.
>
> It has been so long since I have rec'd a letter from So. Ca. that I scarcely know anything that is going on there – probably you have been more fortunate, if so – please let me know what you think of the crisis, and what you intend doing in the event of our State seceding? – It is right that we go together – and I yield to your superior judgement and Experience to guide me in this matter.
>
> I will be here in Vera Cruz all the winter. Write me here by return mail what you intend to do, in case there is a disruption of the Union – or South Carolina secedes. From all accounts it appears that she is going out alone – and it is probable that she will not be followed immediately by any other Southern state. We will find ourselves then in an embarrasing [sic] situation, and I want to know what you are going to do if she secedes alone. Neither of us could ever be found in arms against her, and when the question is reduced to that issue there will be no choice – our destiny will be that of the people with whom it has pleased God to cast our lot, and we will live to enjoy the Glory and honor of Carolina or die in her defence.
>
> This is a very serious question, and I have had long and earnest reflections on it. I thought I would write you and ask your advice – before I acted, and not be precipitate in anything I might do.[5]

All the while South Carolina was taking the necessary steps toward secession. The people were determined to resist the election of Lincoln. The legislature that met on November 5, 1860, to elect presidential electors remained in session until the results of the national election could be ascertained. When it appeared certain that Lincoln was elected, the legislature on November 12 passed a bill calling for a convention to discuss South Carolina's possible withdrawal from the Union.

Among the delegates who met in Columbia on December 17, was Chesley D. Evans of Marion, brother of Captain Evans and an ardent secessionist.[6] Because of an epidemic of smallpox the convention adjourned to Charleston, where on December 20, 1860, the ordinance of secession was unanimously passed. Chesley D. Evans later declared that affixing his name to the ordinance of secession was the proudest act of his life.[7]

The time was approaching when Captain Evans also would have to cast his lot. He could join his family and state or remain in the United States Army which was dear to his heart. While stationed at Camp Cooper, he learned of the withdrawal of South Carolina from the Union and made his decision promptly. Obtaining a leave of absence on January 29, 1861, he left Camp Cooper, never to return. Evans immediately submitted his resignation to the War Department in Washington. In the same mail he wrote to Governor F. W. Pickens of South Carolina offering his services to the state.[8]

As Captain Evans and his wife took leave of their friends in Texas, Robert E. Lee made the following remarks to Vic which she never forgot: "Mrs. Evans, Goodbye. I suppose that they will make your husband a General when you reach home."[9] Evans proceeded to Montgomery, Alabama, where the Confederate Congress was in session, to tender his services to the Confederacy. Upon arriving in Montgomery, he received notice that his resignation had been accepted by the United States government to take effect from February 27. The document was signed by Samuel Cooper, adjutant-general of the United States Army, who was soon to hold the same position in the Confederate Army.[10] On the very day that Evans's resignation was accepted in Washington, Governor Pickens commissioned him adjutant-general of the regular enlisted forces of South Carolina, with the rank of major.[11]

Evans left Montgomery for South Carolina to assume his new duties. Shortly after his arrival in Cokesbury, South Carolina, on March 14, his wife gave birth to a son, who was christened Nathan George. Although elated over becoming a father, the veteran soldier could not remain with his family long. He assumed his duties as adjutant-general on March 28, 1861, when he was sworn in by S. R. Gist.[12]

After South Carolina withdrew from the Union, it took possession of all federal property within the state with the exception of Fort Sumter, where Major Robert Anderson was in command of a garrison of United States troops. Negotiations had been in process since December 1860, with little satisfaction to either side over the question of turning over Fort Sumter to South Carolina. After repeated and unsuccessful demands to evacuate the fort had been made upon both Anderson and the federal government, Confederate officials became convinced that Fort Sumter was going to be reinforced.

General P. G. T. Beauregard, in command of the Confederates at Charleston, obtained intelligence on April 11 that ships were gathering outside the bar to reinforce Anderson. At 3:20 A.M. on the twelfth, he notified Anderson that he would give him one hour in which to leave the fort. Upon Anderson's refusal, the South Carolina batteries opened fire at 4:30 A.M. from Fort Johnson located on James Island. After thirty-four hours of bombardment, Anderson surrendered. The casualties of the bombardment were slight, with only four of the defenders of the fort slightly wounded. Fort Sumter was turned over to the Confederates at 4:00 on the afternoon of April 14.

During the bombardment of Fort Sumter, Major Evans was serving under General R. G. M. Dunovant as adjutant-general of his staff. He had accompanied Dunovant to Sullivan's Island on April 9, and became ill soon afterward. He remained in bed until the beginning of the hostilities, when he joined Dunovant and fulfilled the duties of his post.[13]

By this time a number of volunteer companies had arrived in Charleston. One of these was composed of students from South Carolina College. They had organized at the college and elected

John Hillary Gary, brother-in-law of Major Evans, as their captain. The college officials refused to grant them leave, giving as their reason that the students' services were not needed in Charleston. Nevertheless, the students rebelled against this decision and departed for Charleston.[14]

The day after Anderson's evacuation of Fort Sumter, Evans, jubilant over the victory, enthusiastically wrote to his wife: "Fort Sumter has been burned by our batteries. I think the war is nearly at an end. We have not *lost a single man* no one wounded an unheard of victory – I will be compelled to stay a day or two on the Island in the haste and excitement of victory. I send you a fragment of the Palmetto Flag as shattered by the enemy."[15]

Evans proved to be a poor prophet. Lincoln, soon after the bombardment of Fort Sumter, issued a call for seventy-five thousand troops. This action provoked the secession of Virginia, Arkansas, North Carolina, and Tennessee, thus bringing the number of states to eleven that composed the Southern Confederacy. With the secession of Virginia it was evident that the Old Dominion would be the battleground, and soon volunteers from the different states of the lower South were on their way to Virginia.

Evans, on sick leave at Marion Court House, mentioned this in a May 5 letter to his mother-in-law, Mrs. Thomas R. Gary. Vic and the "little general" had arrived safely, he wrote, but they had had a long and tiresome trip. The railroad cars were overcrowded by the great number of volunteers on their way to Virginia. He continued: "I am gradually improving and think I will be able to return to duty in three days . . . . Everybody is talking of war. I fear I will not be able to go to Virginia unless we have an invasion. You no doubt have seen that John and his Company have been sent back to Columbia. The Governor was very complimentary to the Company."[16]

Evans departed in early May for Montgomery, Alabama, to discuss the disposition of the South Carolina troops with President Jefferson Davis. Governor Pickens wrote to Davis on May 13, stating that Adjutant-General Evans was going to ask the Confederate president to give Evans the necessary orders concerning South Carolina's troops.[17]

While in Montgomery on May 16, Evans received several telegrams from Pickens regarding South Carolina's troops. From the orders, it appeared that the South Carolina regiments were to be disbanded into companies before being inducted into the Confederate Army. This caused Pickens some anxiety because it left South Carolina defenseless.[18]

Evans was back in Charleston on May 20, and received the following orders by telegraph from Samuel Cooper, the adjutant-general of the Confederate Army: "Report to Genl Beauregard for duty in mustering in the S. C. volunteers." On the same day, Evans's commission as major of cavalry was sent to him from Montgomery.[19]

Evans assumed his new duties and began mustering into the Confederate service the various companies. On June 4, he inspected the 7th Regiment of South Carolina Volunteers and inducted them into the army. This regiment, consisting of more than eight hundred men, left for Virginia the same night.[20]

Evans left for Richmond, Virginia, soon thereafter. On June 18, he was ordered to accompany the 4th Regiment of South Carolina Volunteers to Manassas Junction; after making a verbal report of the instructions given him he was to return to Richmond. On the twentieth, Evans returned to Manassas and reported to Beauregard as ordered by General Robert E. Lee: "Major N. G. Evans C.S. Cavalry will proceed without delay to Manassas Junction and report to Brigr. General Beauregard for duty with the cavalry under his command."[21]

The next day Beauregard instructed Evans:

> Proceed with Col. Sloan's Regt. to conduct it to Leesburg, Va., to report to Col. Eppa Hunton Provl. Army C. S., who will employ it to the best advantage in defending that important position, & in preventing the enemy from crossing the Potomac for the purpose of attacking it. You will return to this place via Centreville, & the route Col. Hunton will point out to you, as the one most probable an enemy might follow in a march on this position – scanning carefully such obstacles as might be taken advantage of to delay him, or check him altogether – Col. H. will

afford you all the necessary information & facilities for such a reconnaissance.[22]

Although outranked by both J. B. E. Sloan and Hunton, Evans was evidently put in command of the forces in Leesburg. This is clear from the instructions issued to Evans from the headquarters of the Army of the Potomac on June 26:

> The General was much pleased to hear of the course of Colonels Hunton and Sloan. He feels assured too that you will so exercise the delicate function devolved upon you by the patriotic conduct of these gentlemen, and maintain such relations with them, so as to put out of sight the anomalous position you are placed in.
>
> You should freely consult the views of Col. Hunton, whose knowledge of the country will be of constant use in your operations, and whose previous discharge of his duties have evinced military aptitude.
>
> The General desires you to read the several letters of instructions from these Head Quarters, touching the line of operations he wishes followed by the troops now under his command.
>
> Should he be able to spare another regiment, as he hopes, it will be sent to occupy a point at or near "Gum Springs," or to support your command. . . .[23]

Evans remained at Leesburg until the middle of July, when he received orders to take the 4th South Carolina Regiment back to Manassas. There he would soon make his name.[24]

— Chapter IV —

BULL RUN

The long-expected march of the United States Army toward Richmond commenced on July 16, 1861, when General Irwin McDowell and some thirty thousand troops departed from the banks of the Potomac opposite Washington. The route chosen went by Centreville and Manassas Junction where the Confederate Army under General P. G. T. Beauregard was stationed. After two days of slow marching, the Federal army took possession of the outlying Confederate posts at Fairfax Court House and Centreville, the latter only a few miles from Manassas Junction. The Confederates, offering little resistance, retired across Bull Run and fortified themselves along the banks of that stream.

Bull Run rises in the foothills of the Blue Ridge and meanders slowly to the southeast until it empties into the Occoquan, which flows into the Potomac some forty miles below Alexandria. Bull Run, though, has the volume of a river because of the tidal waters which extend to Union Mills. The Union army advancing from Centreville to Manassas would have to pass between the ford at Sudley Springs and the Occoquan, a distance of fourteen miles, or make an indirect journey around either of those points. Between those points the banks of the stream were steep and for the most part thickly wooded, while the bottom of the creek was muddy except for several fords. The only other crossing was a stone bridge where the Warrenton Turnpike crossed the stream about a mile or so below Sudley Springs. Manassas Junction, situated about midway between the Occoquan and Sudley Springs, was several miles across Bull Run from Centreville.

Beauregard, realizing the advantages that the stream afforded him, stationed his troops along its banks from Union Mills to the stone bridge. He divided his army into seven brigades and assigned Evans, who had arrived with Sloan's South Carolina regiment from Leesburg on July 17, to the command of the 7th Brigade. Evans's command consisted of Sloan's 4th South Carolina Regiment, Wheat's Louisiana Battalion, and two companies of Virginia cavalry. It was the duty of this brigade, which held Beauregard's left flank, to protect the stone bridge crossing.[1]

Upon learning of the Federal advance on July 17, Beauregard urgently telegraphed the army headquarters in Richmond to request more troops. They replied that heavy reinforcements were being sent immediately and instructed him to notify General Joseph E. Johnston to join him at Manassas if practicable. General Theophilus H. Holmes's command at Fredericksburg was also ordered to Manassas.

On the morning of July 18, McDowell ordered General Daniel Tyler to advance with his division along the Warrenton Turnpike toward the stone bridge — but to give the impression that he was advancing on Manassas. Tyler was specifically warned not to bring on an engagement, but to impress upon the Confederates that the Federal advance would be made in that direction. In the meantime, McDowell rode to his left to reconnoiter the terrain and to see if it would be feasible to turn the Confederate right by a flanking movement. His ride disclosed that a flanking movement in this direction would not be advisable because of the roughness of the terrain and other obstacles.[2]

Tyler's advance guard under Colonel I. B. Richardson reached Centreville at nine o'clock. Richardson, instead of taking the Warrenton Road to the stone bridge, took the south road leading directly toward Manassas. Tyler continued to advance until his troops reached the edge of the Centreville ridge where it dips down toward Bull Run. Seeing the Confederates in the distance at Blackburn's Ford, Tyler decided to attack. In the engagement that followed the Confederates under the able leadership of Brigadier-General James Longstreet held their position. Late in the afternoon the Federals retired.

Convinced that a flanking movement around the Confederate right was impracticable, McDowell spent the nineteenth and twentieth in reconnaissance of the terrain adjoining the Confederate left. He finally decided on the afternoon of the twentieth to turn the Confederates left.

The two-day delay in the attack gave Beauregard's reinforcements time to arrive. Upon receiving General Samuel Cooper's telegram at 1:00 A.M. on the eighteenth telling of Beauregard's plight, Johnston immediately prepared to leave Winchester, Virginia, for Manassas. Believing that General Robert Patterson was determined not to move on him, Johnston departed with his army about noon on the eighteenth. He reached Manassas about midday on the twentieth, most of his army having preceded him. One brigade, however, under the command of E. Kirby Smith, was still at Piedmont awaiting transportation. Johnston was notified by President Davis before he reached Manassas that he had been promoted to general, which made him the superior officer on the field.

As soon as he arrived, Johnston went to see Beauregard. He informed Beauregard of the possibility of Patterson's troops joining McDowell in the immediate future and advised an attack at once. Beauregard had formed the same opinion and showed Johnston the position of the troops. Believing that General Winfield Scott had ordered the Federal army to advance at Mitchell's Ford, he had concentrated his strength to the east of it. Beauregard had positioned his troops in the following fashion: Richard Ewell's brigade was at Union Mills Ford with its left extending toward McLean's Ford; Holmes's brigade was placed a short distance to the rear of Ewell's; D. R. Jones's brigade was located in front of McLean's Ford and extended from Ewell's brigade to Longstreet's brigade at Blackburn's Ford; Jubal Early's brigade was placed in the rear as a support; N. L. Bonham's brigade at Mitchell's Ford extended from Longstreet's left to Cooke's right;

T. J. Jackson's brigade supported Longstreet, while the brigades of Barnard E. Bee and F. S. Bartow were stationed along a pine thicket at equal distance from Blackburn's and McLean's Fords; Phillip St. George Cooke's brigade protected Island, Ball's, and Lewis' Fords; Evans's brigade guarded the stone bridge and a farm ford about a mile around the bridge; J. E. B. Stuart's cavalry was placed in the rear of Bonham and Cooke and two companies of R. C. W. Radford's cavalry were stationed in the rear of Mitchell's Ford.[3]

Beauregard pointed out to Johnston on the maps the five possible roads the Confederates could take to Centreville. The troops then were to be concentrated near the Federal camps. Johnston concurred in the plan and, since he had had little sleep in three nights, gave Beauregard authority to issue the orders. Beauregard was late in writing out the orders which were to be sent to the different brigade commanders. When the orders reached Johnston to be signed, it was nearly daybreak.[4]

In the meantime, McDowell at Centreville had completed his plans. After deciding to make a flanking movement around the Confederate left, he gave orders accordingly. General David Hunter's division was to leave at 2:00 A.M. on the twenty-first from Centreville on the Warrenton Turnpike. After passing Cub Run, Hunter was to turn to the right and pass Bull Run above the lower ford at Sudley Springs. Hunter was then to turn to his left and clear away the Confederate forces guarding the lower ford and the stone bridge. After accomplishing this, he was to bear to his right and make room for the divisions that followed. General Samuel P. Heintzelman's division was to follow at 2:30 A.M. and cross the lower ford after Hunter had cleared it. Tyler's division was to move on the stone bridge at the same hour, but was not to open fire until daybreak. Dixon S. Miles's division, supported by Richardson's brigade, was to protect Centreville and threaten the Confederates at Blackburn's Ford, but they were instructed only to make a demonstration with their artillery.[5]

The plans of attack were carefully explained to the Federal division and brigade commanders when they assembled on the night of the twentieth. The meeting was not altogether cheerful because the Union army was showing signs of demoralization. Two commands had already obtained their release from service from McDowell because of the expiration of their enlistment.

At 3:00 A.M. the following morning, Robert C. Schenck's brigade led the movement of Tyler's division advancing slowly along the Warrenton Turnpike. As soon as Schenck reached the junction of the Sudley Springs road about 5:00 A.M., he fired a few shells in the direction of the stone bridge; receiving no response, he advanced carefully. He finally arrived at a position about a thousand yards from the bridge and deployed to the left. Following Schenck, William T. Sherman's brigade moved to the right. E. D. Keyes's brigade followed and halted between the line Tyler had deployed and the junction of the Sudley Springs road and the turnpike. As Keyes cleared the junction, Hunter's and Heintzelman's division started their long, circuitous route to Sudley Springs. They left the junction at 6:00 A.M., which was the time that McDowell had planned for them to be at Sudley Springs.

Colonel Evans, stationed at the stone bridge about two miles below the Sudley Springs Ford, was considerably separated from the rest of the line. According to Beauregard's plans, Evans's brigade was apparently left out of the impending hostilities, much to Evans's dismay. This, however, did not prove to be true.

At 5:15 A.M. the Federal batteries began to shell Evans's position from a distance of about fifteen hundred yards. The batteries continued their fire at intervals for about an hour. Since Evans's forces were well protected by the crest of the hill on the west side of the bridge, he did not return their fire. Evans immediately notified Beauregard that he had been shelled and that the Federals had deployed some twelve hundred men in his front. That was all that Evans could see of Tyler's division of over nine thousand men. Beauregard sent orders to Evans and General Phillip St. George Cooke to hold their positions to the last extremity. Upon Johnston's request, Beauregard ordered Bee's and Jackson's brigades to the left near the stone bridge and also instructed Colonel Wade Hampton, who had just arrived with his Legion, to proceed to the same locality.[6]

Beauregard decided to change the place of his attack. He recommended to Johnston an attack by the Confederate right wing and center on the Federal flank. Johnston approved the plans, and Beauregard proceeded to issue the necessary orders. The six brigades of the Confederate right were to strike the flank of the troops attacking Evans at the bridge, while Cooke's, Jackson's, and Bee's brigades and Wade Hampton's Legion were meeting their assault. But these orders, like the first, were rendered useless because of the delay in delivering them.[7]

In the meantime, the Federal skirmishers were advancing on Evans in considerable force. He directed two companies of Sloan's regiment and one of Wheat's battalion to advance so as to cover his front. The skirmishers were sent out and reached the bank of Bull Run, where they deployed on each side of the bridge. The Federal troops could be seen in the opposite woods. At intervals the Federal batteries fired over the heads of the Confederate skirmishers in order to make them show their position, which was concealed. The skirmishers kept up a fire for over an hour, and Evans soon became convinced that Tyler would not advance upon his front. About this time Dr. Bronaugh, one of Evans's men, with a courier from Captain E. P. Alexander, brought Evans word that McDowell had turned Evans's flank and was moving with a strong force around the Confederate rear to Manassas. Evans had a great decision to make. Should he remain at the bridge as ordered or meet this advance with his small body of soldiers? Although Evans had no instructions as to what to do in such an emergency, he did not hesitate. He sent word to Cooke that he was turned and that he was going to meet the Federal flanking movement. Leaving four companies to guard his former position at the bridge, Evans departed with six companies of Sloan's regiment, Wheat's battalion, two 6-pounders of Latham's Battery, and a company of cavalry under one Captain R. Terry to meet McDowell's flanking column of two divisions.[8]

Guided by Dr. Bronaugh, who was familiar with the terrain, Evans moved near the Carter house, where he temporarily stationed his troops. From the rising ground north of Sudley Springs the Federal commanders saw the Confederates coming into position about a mile away. General Ambrose Burnside leading the

Northern advance crossed at Sudley Springs and started on the road to Manassas. Evans then changed positions and moved in a southwesterly direction until he reached the Manassas-Sudley Springs road. He wisely decided not to place his troops across the road, but judiciously selected a position flanking it. This gave his command a wide zone of fire on its front while its right was protected by woods. His line of battle was formed at right angles to his former line and not only blocked the Manassas-Sudley Springs road, but also put up a determined front to any Federal advance to the Confederate left and rear. To Evans's rear and to the south was Young's branch, whose banks rose into a plateau where the Robinson and Henry houses were situated.[9]

Along this line Evans's band of about nine hundred men was stationed with the 4th South Carolina Regiment under Colonel J. B. E. Sloan on the left with one gun, and Major Robert Wheat on the right supported by Terry's company of cavalry. Evans instructed his command to fire as soon as the enemy came within musket range.[10]

When Burnside advanced, he was promptly met by a terrific fire from Sloan's regiment. Soon afterward Wheat countercharged and the 27th New York broke. Evans held his own for more than an hour, but as the Federals kept sending in reinforcements, it proved too much for his thin line. Having already sent for reinforcements, this brave little band had held back the Northern onslaught long enough for Bee, Colonel F. S. Bartow, and the Hampton Legion to form a line of battle on the Henry Hill. Evans, however, was too hotly engaged to withdraw, so he sent word to Bee by one of his staff officers to come to his rescue. Bee went promptly to his old friend's aid. He sent Bartow with the 7th and 8th Georgia towards the Carter house and with the rest of the brigade strengthened Evans's wavering line. Bee arrived just as Evans was completely beaten, and all that he could do was to make the best of the predicament that he was in. He put up a strong resistance for some time, but was forced to yield to superior numbers. These troops in retreat, like the majority of the troops engaged in this battle, showed a lack of organization to stand against fire in the open. The Confederate line finally broke and, being constantly sprayed by the batteries, streamed eastward down the turnpike and along the Henry house plateau or climbed up the hill and moved across to descend to the other side. Others followed Young's branch and turned south at the Henry house plateau and joined their broken commands. The officers tried hard to stem the tide, but they were expecting too much of an inexperienced and unprepared army. Consequently, the Confederates paid the price of high expectations. The officers risked their lives aimlessly in stopping the retreat and a number, including Sloan and Wheat, were severely wounded. But Bee and Evans had held long enough to permit Jackson to form along the Henry house plateau.

Evans and Bartow, with a small remnant of their commands, fell back and joined Colonel Wade Hampton, who had stationed his Legion at the Robinson house. When Evans reached Hampton, Hampton asked where his command was. Evans wept; his command was gone. Hampton's Legion fell back to the brow of the hill, but soon he was attacked from the right and his Legion was nearly surrounded. After consulting Bee and Evans, Hampton gave orders to retire and his command re-formed near Imboden's battery along Jackson's line.[11]

Johnston and Beauregard reached the Henry house plateau about 12:30 P.M. and were met by Bee's and Evans's troops in full retreat. Johnston rallied remnants of the troops and placed the 4th Alabama under the command of Colonel S. R. Gist and four other companies under Colonel F. J. Thomas. It was during this part of the engagement that Bee is said to have given Jackson the name of "Stonewall." The presence of Beauregard and Johnston with the troops under fire and the assurance of aid seemed to restore the spirits of the fleeing troops.[12]

With the new line now formed upon Jackson's brigade and with troops coming from the fords reinforcing the line, the Confederates were able to check the Federal advance. The battle see-sawed until about three o'clock in the afternoon, when Beauregard received a signal from the hills to watch out for an enemy advance from his left. Beauregard raised his glasses, but since the troops were over a mile away could not recognize their standards. At the time, the only person with Beauregard was Colonel Evans, his staff having been sent away to carry dispatches. Later, Beauregard would confide that "To [Evans], I communicated my doubts and my fears. I told him that I feared the approaching force was in reality Patterson's division; that if such was the case, I would be compelled to fall back on my reserves, and postpone, until the next day, a continuation of the engagement."[13] Turning to Evans, Beauregard directed him to go to Johnston and ask him to collect his reserves so as to protect a retreat. Evans had gone but a short distance when Beauregard looked again at the approaching troops, and this time he discovered that they were carrying the Stars and Bars of the Confederacy. At the same time an orderly reached him. "'Col. Evans,' exclaimed Beauregard, his face lighting up, 'ride forward and order General Kirby Smith to hurry up his command, and strike them on the flank and rear.'"[14]

The arrival of Smith's brigade was the turning point of the battle. The Federals had already advanced on Jackson in the center of the new line and were met not only with a strong volley but by a counter-charge. Smith's brigade struck the Federal flank and then Beauregard ordered a general advance. The Northern troops were driven over the Henry house plateau. McDowell endeavored to stop the movement by throwing in General O. O. Howard's brigade, but it was unable to stop the Confederates. The Confederates, now firing Northern artillery as well as their own, quickly cleared the field of Federal troops.

McDowell made a last stand at Young's branch. He re-formed his line, but this failed to stop the Southerners, who were now reinforced by Jubal Early's brigade. Again the Federal right was thrown back and Beauregard swept toward Mathew's Hill. This time the Federal army broke completely. The Confederate infantry was in no condition to pursue, but the cavalry was, and in no time the Federal retreat became a panic. The cavalry was soon overburdened with the large numbers of prisoners taken and this encumbered its use. At Centreville, the Federal reserves held as darkness approached, but thousands of Northern soldiers continued their flight to Washington pursued only by their fears.

The Confederates had won a great victory, but Colonel Evans could not rejoice. Upon the red battlefield his lifelong friend had fallen. Evans never forgot this true friend and great soldier who came to his aid when so badly needed. Several years later he named one of his sons Barnard Bee, in remembrance of him.

Evans received from his immediate superiors restrained praise for his services during the battle of Bull Run. General Johnston in his report said: ". . . he was attacked by the enemy in immensely superior numbers, against which he maintained himself with skill and unshrinking courage . . . Our victory was complete . . . It is due . . . to . . . the admirable conduct of . . . Colonel (commanding brigades) Evans, . . ." While Beauregard in his report stated: "Evans and his men had maintained their stand with almost matchless tenacity . . . It is fit that I should in this way commend to notice the dauntless conduct and imperturbable coolness of Colonel Evans."[15]

There were others on the field that day who also praised him. Colonel St. George Cooke in his report of the battle stated:

> The Major [Evans} promptly and heroically turned to meet him with his entire force . . . Never perhaps in the history of modern warfare was there so unequal a contest as now ensued. With his small but heroic numbers Major Evans advanced to fight the head of a column of 25,000 men, amongst whom were some of the best regiments of the Federal army, strengthened by numerous batteries of well-appointed artillery of the most improved kind. For more than an hour this contest was maintained without assistance, . . . I deem it proper to state that the conduct of Majors Evans and Wheat is above all praise.[16]

Brevet Major-General James B. Fry, U.S.A., who was captain and assistant adjutant-general on McDowell's staff during the battle, said: "Evans' action was probably one of the best pieces of soldiership on either side during the campaign, but it seems to have received no special commendation from his superiors."[17]

General Fitzhugh Lee praised Evans even further:

> "Shanks" Evans, as he was called, was a graduate of the Military Academy, a native South Carolinian [who] served in the celebrated old 2nd Dragoons, and was a good type of the rip-

roaring, scorn-all-care element, which abounded so largely in that regiment. He has never received the credit to which he was so justly entitled in this battle. It was fighting his handful of men to a frazzle that enabled the Confederate commanders to change their line of battle, and form a new line to retard the Federal flanking force, and his action, as will be seen, was based upon his own responsibility. Evans had the honor of opening the fight, we may say, fired the first gun of war. With his little line of battle, made up of 700 soldiers, he marched away to fight McDowell's turning column of over 18,000. It was a brave little line but accomplished its purpose; for over an hour he held in check the overwhelming forces of the enemy, until Jackson and Hampton could arrive to save the day.[18]

N. W. Brooker, who fought under Evans for a while during the war, spoke without equivocation about Shanks's role in the battle:

> The writer was with that brave man a while and knew his merits and qualifications and can speak with compliments of him . . .The further fact is that no writer as far as I have ever seen has ever written what I regard as full justice of General Evans as to his part in that decisive conflict [Bull Run] . . . Evans stationed at Stone bridge with 11 companies rapidly threw his command up the creek, confronting the enemy who were flanking and crossing the river above – 16,000 strong – and held them, holding his ground nobly (indefinitely) until Gen. Bee advanced to the rescue only after Evans' force was swept out of existence by the over-whelming odds. . . .The truth is Evans intended to die with his brave men upon the spot . . . No braver man ever lived than N. G. Evans. Never a more enthusiastic, determined soldier and fighter seeming always to court death.[19]

— *Chapter V* —

LEESBURG

After its defeat on July 21, the Federal army fell back in full retreat toward Washington. On the twenty-second, Beauregard advanced his corps to new positions. His new line now extended from a mile above the stone bridge on Bull Run on the left to Union Mills on the right. Bonham's brigade was stationed in the front at Centreville, while Evans's command was again assigned to a position near the stone bridge.[1]

On July 25, Beauregard reorganized the Army of the Potomac [Confederate]. He divided his corps into eight brigades and several detachments of troops. Evans was again assigned to the command of the 7th Brigade, which was composed of the 13th, 17th, and 18th Mississippi regiments under the leadership of Colonels William Barksdale, W. S. Featherston, and E. R. Burt, respectively.[2]

Although Evans had been in command of several regiments of troops for over a month and had been ranked as a colonel by his superiors at the front, he did not receive official notice of his promotion from the headquarters of the army in Richmond until July 26. On that day, General Cooper notified Beauregard that N. G. Evans had been temporarily assigned to the rank of colonel, but that if an emergency arose, he could assign Evans to a higher rank. Assistant Adjutant-General Thomas Jordan immediately wrote Evans: "A dispatch from Gen Cooper to the General this afternoon announced that you had been made a Colonel of the Provisional Army & thus would be eligible to command a Brigade. You are therefore assigned to the 7th Brigade as you will see by the order herewith."[3]

Evans had written to General Robert E. Lee on July 11, requesting Lee to aid him in getting a promotion to brigadier-general. Evans, no doubt, thought that his past experience in the United States Army entitled him to a higher rank; especially so, since some of the brigade commanders in the Confederate army had had very little, if any, military experience. Still, others who had held the same or lower rank in the United States Army before secession outranked him in the Confederate army, and this rankled Evans. Lee replied to his letter two weeks later: "I have not ansd. your letter of the 11th. because I could not make the arrangements you desired. It will only be postponed a little while I hope, you are now a Colonel, [you] Can command your brigade, & will soon give cause I know for the advancement of the other step."[4]

For nearly three weeks the 7th Brigade remained in the vicinity of Manassas. Every day both officers and men anticipated orders that would start them on an offensive against Washington. This idea was soon abandoned, and on August 11, 1861, Colonel Evans's brigade was ordered to Leesburg to increase the force there and also to give the ailing Mississippians an opportunity to recover in that country. Evans's brigade was now composed of the three Mississippi regiments, Hunton's 8th Virginia, two companies of cavalry, and a battery of Richmond howitzers.[5]

The Mississippi troops were among the finest in the army. Most of the men were bear hunters from the swamps and canebrakes of their native state and were as tough as the bears they hunted. As could be expected from the outdoor life that they led, the Mississippians, hardly without exception, were excellent marksmen. Their enthusiasm was irrepressible; laughter, shouting, singing, or the Rebel yell burst indifferently from their lips. It was a common saying during the war that the sick man in Barksdale's camp made more noise than any full regiment in the army.

At this time, Leesburg was perhaps the most desirable post in the Confederate lines because of the character of its country and people. The latter were very hospitable and shared almost all they had with the soldiers, while the former was beautiful and fertile, providing for the needs of both man and beast. The ladies of the town did their utmost to make the soldiers welcome by giving numerous entertainments for them.[6]

While Colonel Evans was enjoying the hospitality of this town, heart-rending news reached him from his Carolina home. His mother, Jane Beverly Evans, was accidentally killed on September 3, while inspecting some repairs on the roof of her residence in Marion. One of her slaves who was doing carpentry work, not seeing anyone below, dropped a stick of timber that struck Mrs. Evans on the head. She survived only a few hours. The slave, who received no punishment, was so heartbroken over the accident that he is reputed to have lost his mind. Mrs. Evans's death was a shock not only to her immediate family, but also to a large circle of friends. Her hospitality was a byword along the Pee Dee. She was a friend to the unfortunate, always endeavoring to do her best to make their lives more comfortable. For years it had been her custom every Sunday morning to send her butler, "Old Henry," with a tray laden with the delicacies of her breakfast table for the prisoners at the county jail.[7]

Although Evans was grief-stricken, he remained at his post of duty. The Confederates stationed at Leesburg were now facing the possibility of a Federal attack. Since the battle of Bull Run, the Federal authorities, fearing an attack upon Washington from the vicinity of Leesburg, had fortified heavily the Maryland banks of the Potomac from Harpers Ferry to Washington. After a time, since the prospect of a Confederate invasion did not materialize, the Federal army changed its policy from the defensive to the offensive, with Leesburg as its immediate objective.[8]

During this time, Evans had been regularly drilling his troops so that they might be prepared for whatever might happen. He had kept an alert watch on the Federal activities across the Potomac and had sent out numerous scouting parties to discover their plans. The Federal batteries continually fired across the river in order to shell the Confederates from their positions. This fire was returned by the Richmond howitzers. During these engagements, several Confederates were killed and a number wounded.[9]

On September 25, Beauregard, anticipating a Federal offensive, sent Evans the following instructions: "The enemy is threatening our front – be prepared for any offensive movement against you – in which case, you will act as already instructed – delay his march as long as practicable – but be careful not to be out off from your line of retreat – We can at present send you no reinforcements."[10]

In the meantime Beauregard had been planning to reorganize his corps, which meant the exchange of the Mississippi regiments of which Evans was particularly proud. On October 6, Beauregard wrote to Evans concerning this matter: "As I soon may have to make a new combination of commands I will not carry into effect the exchange of those two Regts. I intended to make – At any rate I will wait awhile longer – the 13th however (if not all the others) will be put under Genl. Clark who has applied for them all with a strong show of reason."[11]

As yet Evans had not been promoted to brigadier-general. On October 8, he wrote to Beauregard concerning his promotion and the disposition of the Mississippi regiments. Beauregard replied the following day:

> Your favor of yesterday rec'd. With regard to your appt. I have said and written on the subject *all* that I could, but rec'd. no definite answer – A short while ago, Genl. J. [Johnston] & myself, sent in a list of new Brigadiers with your name on it –
>
> As to the command of the Mississippi Regts., Genl. Clark claims them & the Pres't. approves of it. Such a change of comm's. would necessarily involve a change of Station, altho' I am fully aware of all the advantages we have in keeping you there – But these new promotions whenever made will necessitate several changes of stations and commands – but I hope to give you as fine a Brigade (if not better) than your present one.[12]

The proposed change of regiments or station not having taken place, Evans continued in command at Leesburg. On October 17, Evans, believing a flank movement by the Northern army was forthcoming along the Aldie turnpike (which ran from Alexandria to Snickersville Gap in the Blue Ridge Mountains), retired to

Carter's Hill some five miles from Leesburg. He reported his retreat to Beauregard. Jordan instantly replied on the same day:

> Your note of this day has been laid before the general, who wishes to be informed of the reasons that influenced you to take up your present position, as you omit to inform him. The point you occupy is understood to be very strong, and the General hopes you will be able to maintain it against odds should the enemy press across the river and move in this direction. To prevent such a movement and junction of Banks' forces with McClellan's is of utmost military importance, and you will be expected to make a desperate stand, falling back only in the face of an overwhelming enemy. In case, unfortunately you should be obliged to retire, march on this point and effect a juncture with his corps.
>
> If you still deem it best to remain at Carter's Mill, the general desires you to maintain possession of Leesburg as an outpost by a regiment without baggage or tents, and to be relieved every three or four days.[13]

Upon receipt of the instructions, Evans immediately marched his force back to Leesburg. He assigned the three Mississippi regiments between the burnt bridge over Goose Creek and Edwards' Ferry, which is below Leesburg near the mouth of Goose Creek. The remainder of the brigade he located at Leesburg.[14]

The principal points now held by the Confederates on the Virginia side of the Potomac above Washington were Dranesville, Leesburg, and Charleston. In order to determine the Confederate forces at Dranesville, General George B. McClellan ordered General George A. McCall, who was in command of a division stationed just above Washington, to make a reconnaissance toward Dranesville. McCall successfully carried out his assignment, occupying Dranesville on October 19. Meeting no opposition, he deployed his skirmishers as far as Goose Creek.[15]

About seven o'clock on the night of the nineteenth, the Federal batteries began to shell Evans's entrenchments at Fort Evans, on the Leesburg turnpike, and at Edwards' Ferry. The Confederates also heard heavy firing near Dranesville. At midnight Evans ordered his entire brigade to the burnt bridge, having heard that the

Federals were advancing in that direction in full force. Evans selected a strong position on the north side of the creek and there waited for the Federal advance. Looking for an attack by a superior force, Evans had already dispatched a letter to Beauregard for reinforcements.[16]

On the morning of the twentieth the Confederates captured a courier who was carrying messages from McCall to General George G. Meade, requesting Meade to examine the roads to Leesburg. By interrogating the captured soldier, Evans ascertained the position of the troops at Dranesville.[17]

By noon that day, Beauregard wrote to Evans:

> Your letter of yesterday has been received. We will not be able to re-enforce you without weakening this point too much – hence you must act as already instructed. We may be able to attack the Enemy in flank towards Drainsville [sic].
>
> You are requested to cause your patrols to meet those of Radfords if practicable as suggested by Genl. Stuart to Col. Jennifer [sic]. We are all working for one object the safety of our country.[18]

In the meantime, on October 20, McClellan notified General Charles P. Stone, in command of a Federal division stationed at Poolesville, Maryland, across the Potomac from Leesburg, that McCall had occupied Dranesville and would that day send out reconnaissances from his station. McClellan instructed Stone: "Keep a good lookout upon Leesburg, to see if this movement has the effect to drive them away. Perhaps a slight demonstration on your part would have the effect to move them."[19]

After receiving McClellan's orders, Stone went at 1:00 P.M. with General Willis A. Gorman's brigade to Edwards' Ferry, dispatching at the same time four companies of troops under Colonel Charles Devens to Harrison's Island. Colonels W. Raymond Lee and Milton Cogswell with their regiments and a section of battery were sent to Conrad's Ferry at the end of Harrison's Island, where part of a battery had already been stationed.

During the afternoon Stone made a demonstration at Edwards' Ferry and forced a Confederate regiment that had appeared to retire. That night Stone obtained information that Leesburg was poorly guarded from the direction of Harrison's Island at Ball's Bluff. He then ordered Colonel Devens to advance along that route and attack the force at daybreak. To cover this movement, Stone ordered a demonstration at Edwards' Ferry the next morning.[20]

Evans, unaware of the presence of the troops that Stone had sent to his rear during the night and expecting an attack from the direction of Dranesville, had had his men drawn up in a line of battle along Goose Creek before daybreak. He then addressed them: "Gentlemen, the enemy are approaching by the Dranesville road, sixteen thousand strong, with twenty pieces of artillery. They want to cut off our retreat. Reinforcements can't arrive in time if they were sent. We must fight."[21] Obviously, Evans had disregarded Beauregard's order to fall back if he were opposed by overwhelming numbers.

In the meantime, Devens was advancing along the path from Ball's Bluff. He finally encountered the Confederate pickets and drove them in. The pickets reported to Captain W. L. Duff of the 17th Mississippi, who was guarding this route to Leesburg, that the Federals were crossing in large numbers at Harrison's Island. Duff immediately sent a messenger to report these facts to Evans. He then proceeded to meet the Federal attack with his band of forty men and held his position until reinforcements arrived.[22]

In the early dawn hours, Evans, observing the Federal movements from Fort Evans, discovered that the enemy had effected a crossing both at Edwards' Ferry and Ball's Bluff. Evans prepared to meet them. He sent Lieutenant-Colonel Walter Jenifer[23] with four companies of infantry and a cavalry force to support Duff.[24]

Jenifer proceeded to the support of Duff and, upon arriving at the scene of hostilities, took command. He attacked the Federals and drove them from their positions, but realizing that his force was too small to take the offensive, he retired behind a fence and sent for reinforcements.[25]

At ten o'clock Evans became convinced that the real attack was at Ball's Bluff and dispatched Colonel Eppa Hunton's 8th Virginia Regiment to Jenifer's rescue. Before Hunton left, Evans directed him to form in the rear of Jenifer's command and to drive the enemy into the river. He also assured Hunton that he would support him with artillery. Hunton joined Jenifer about twelve o'clock.[26]

In the meantime, Colonel Edward D. Baker had assumed leadership of the Federal forces with about two thousand soldiers under his direction. He had stationed them in a thick body of woods along the crest of a hill that descended to a cleared field of some 450 feet wide and 1,250 feet long surrounded completely by woods. The woods extended back about 125 feet to Ball's Bluff, which declined abruptly to the river. Upon his arrival, Hunton ordered the Virginians to charge through the woods. Although greatly outnumbered, the Confederates drove the Federals from the woods. Baker then formed his line upon the farther side of the cleared field.[27]

At 1:30 P.M., Hunton sent E. V. "Lige" White to Evans for reinforcements. "Tell Hunton to fight on," Evans replied. Hunton's ammunition was nearly exhausted, so he dispatched a note to Evans for a supply, but it failed to arrive. He sent White again at 2:30 P.M. with a message to Evans telling him that if ammunition and reinforcements were not sent immediately he could not hold his position. "Tell Hunton to hold the ground till every damn man falls," answered Evans.[28] He then dispatched the 18th Mississippi to his aid.

At three o'clock Evans, realizing that the Federals were in considerable numbers near Ball's Bluff, ordered Colonel Featherston's 17th Mississippi Regiment to Hunton's support. Featherston immediately hurried to his aid. About 4:00 P.M., Baker, who was out front urging his men on, was pierced by several bullets and instantly killed. Colonel Lee then took command and started to order the Federals to retreat to the rear, but it was soon discovered that Colonel Cogswell was his senior in command. Cogswell decided to march to the left and attempt to cut his way through to Edwards' Ferry. Just as he was making preparations for the march, a member of Evans's staff, Lieutenant Charles B. Wildman, who was slightly intoxicated, happened upon the Federal lines. Mistaking the Federals for Confederates, he pointed out a body of

Confederates and in a very official manner ordered the Federals to charge.[29]

The charge was made by the Tammany Regiment, which pulled the whole Federal line with it. They received a murderous fire from the Confederates at close quarters and retreated. Cogswell recalled the men, but the proposed movement to the left was now out of the question; therefore he gave orders to retire down the bluff. The Federals were hotly pursued by the Confederates and pushed over the bluff at the point of the bayonet. The Confederates, standing at the top of the bluff, poured volley after volley into the Federals, who made a gallant stand at the edge of the river rather than surrender. The Federals, however, soon became panic-stricken and rushed into a large boat, which became overcrowded and sank about fifteen feet from shore. Others threw their weapons into the river and attempted to swim to the Maryland shore; a large number drowned. Around 7:00 P.M. the rout was complete.[30]

During this time Stone was at Edwards' Ferry. At 4:00 P.M. he wired Banks to send him a brigade, which he intended to use as a reserve at Harrison's Island. A little before five o'clock, news reached him of Baker's death. Stone left at once for the banks opposite Harrison's Island and arrived there to see his troops in complete rout. Orders soon arrived from army headquarters for Stone to hold Harrison's Island and the Virginia shore of Edwards' Ferry at all costs and he issued orders to carry these instructions into effect.[31]

Meanwhile, Colonel Cogswell and a number of his men had surrendered at Ball's Bluff. After darkness, "Lige" White and Lieutenant-Colonel John McQuirk led a party of Confederates below the bluff, where they captured 325 more Federals.[32]

Evans had the prisoners marched to Leesburg. He interviewed the Federal commissioned officers and offered them the freedom of the town if they would promise not to take up arms against the Confederacy until duly exchanged. They refused this offer and intimated to Evans that they expected to be released by the Federal army during the night. Evans then decided to send them immediately to Manassas. Captain O. R. Singleton, with two companies of infantry and a cavalry force, safely conducted the 529 prisoners to Manassas, a journey of twenty-five miles.[33]

One of the prisoners informed Evans that the Confederates could not win the war unless they were ready to "wade knee deep in Northern blood." The general replied: "Sir, we shall go breast deep, if necessary; only leave our arms free to cut down our enemies."[34]

Evans ordered his brigade to retire to Leesburg for the night with the exception of the 13th Mississippi, which remained stationed at Edwards' Ferry. The next morning, Evans ordered Barksdale to make an accurate reconnaissance of the Federal position at Edwards' Ferry and then assault it.

At two o'clock in the afternoon of the twenty-third, Barksdale advanced upon the Federals. Although outnumbered and constantly preyed upon by the Federal batteries, the Confederates drove the Federals back of their field works. Barksdale, after holding his position for some time, retired to Fort Evans, which he reached after dark. Both sides claimed they inflicted heavy casualties upon the other, but in reality they lost about two men each.[35]

Evans ordered his brigade to sleep on the battlefield that night in order to attack the Federals the next morning at Edwards' Ferry. The next morning, however, Evans, realizing that his brigade was very much exhausted, instructed them to retire toward Carter's Mill in order to recuperate. He left Barksdale's regiment at Leesburg with two pieces of artillery and a cavalry force to act as an advance guard. He then stationed Hunton's regiment with two pieces of artillery on the south bank of the Sycolin Creek about three miles from Leesburg, and the balance of the troops retired farther down the road. That night McClellan ordered the Federal troops to withdraw from the Virginia shore at Edwards' Ferry and by five o'clock the next morning they had completely evacuated.[36]

Evans gave his losses in the October 21 conflict as 153 killed and wounded and two taken prisoners. He listed the captured Federal property as follows: fifteen hundred stands of arms, a stand of colors, a large number of cartridge boxes, bayonet scabbards, three pieces of cannon, and a quantity of camp furniture. He gave the Federal loss as 1,300 killed, drowned, and wounded and 1,500 prisoners. The Federal returns show, however, that they lost forty-nine killed, 165 wounded and 714 missing.[37]

Evans reported that he was opposed by 8,000 troops at Ball's Bluff and Edwards' Ferry. A fairer estimation of the number engaged would be around 2,000 at Ball's Bluff, not counting those on the Maryland shore and Harrison's Island, and about 2,500 at Edwards' Ferry. Evans also stated in his report that the Confederates had 1,709 men on the field, but only one company of the 13th Mississippi was engaged at Ball's Bluff.[38]

When the news of the Confederate victory at Leesburg reached Beauregard, he urged General Johnston to take the offensive and cut off Stone before he could retire to Maryland. Johnston, however, would not agree to this because he feared that something might occur that would require all the forces with the main army.

Thomas Jordan, assistant adjutant-general of the Confederate army, praised Evans for his performance:

> The General congratulates you heartily for your brilliant success of yesterday and hopes that the enemy have been so worsted that he will not essay another trial of arms with you.
>
> It is not deemed prudent for you to maintain however your position against any desperate odds as Genl. Johnston has decided that he cannot reinforce you sufficiently to enable . . . you to withstand their whole force should the enemy resolve to throw it across. In other words, as before directed – if an overpowering force of the enemy assails you, you are instructed to retire on this army – taking care to follow such a route as shall secure your flank . . . from the quarter of Drainesville [sic].
>
> Two Regiments however will be dispatched in light marching order to support your retreat should that be forced upon you. But these Regiments must return here if on the third day the enemy are indisposed to renew the attack.
>
> Ammunition will also be sent you.
>
> The prisoners and captured artillery ought to be secured by being sent here at once by a way to avoid interception from Drainesville. Turn out the militia for this purpose and call on all good citizens to arm and rally to your standard; it is hoped that the arms captured from the enemy will enable you to arm such – trusting to your good fortune, courage and ability the General

confidently hopes that you will after all have no occasion to abandon your position.

The regiments will march as soon as possible by the Gum Springs road – You should send couriers to meet & direct their march upon such points as you may wish them.[39]

On the morning of October 22, the 5th South Carolina, 8th Louisiana, four pieces of artillery, and a Virginia company of cavalry were sent to Evans's support. The troops reached Genas Creek about six miles from Leesburg that night. They were stationed near Leesburg until the twenty-sixth, when they occupied the town. The menace of the Federal attack having passed, they returned to Manassas on October 28.

The Confederate victory at Leesburg was joyously received by most of the Southern people. On October 22, General Johnston had the following congratulatory orders issued:

> The Commanding General announces to the Army with great Satisfaction a Brilliant Success achieved yesterday near Leesburg by Colonel Evans and his brigade.
>
> After a Contest lasting from early morning until dark, this Brigade routed and drove back into Maryland a very large force. Capturing 6 Cannon and 520 prisoners and killing and wounding a large number.
>
> The Skill and Courage with which this victory has been achieved entitle Colonel Evans and the 7th Brigade of the 1st Corps to the thanks of the Army.[40]

The Southern press praised Evans just as they had at Bull Run. On October 23, "Hermes" wrote from Richmond to the Charleston *Mercury*:

> Three times and a tiger for the heroic South Carolinian, General Evans! I knew the man was game to the backbone the first time I laid eyes on him. He proved it on the day of Manassas when with Sloan's South Carolina Regiment and Wheat's Louisiana Battalion, he kept 12,000 of the enemy at bay for an hour. And now with three regiments and *no artillery*, he has given *Stone* a terrible lambasting, killed Baker, of Oregon, (an excellent

thing,) taken 6 pieces, 800 prisoners, and killed wounded and "drownded" 1,200 more. It is fine — . . . Everybody wants to go to war; and the most cowardly of the stay-at-home-and-play-billiards club are grinning with joy and imaginary valor. Who can't whip the Yankees, now? Mr. Evans, you have done a fine thing. 'Kind sir, we give you thanks.'[41]

"Kiawah" wrote the *Mercury* from the Confederate camp near Centreville:

Sound the bugles, roll the drums, wave the banners, shout out the loudest huzzas, for the gallant Evans and his Spartan band at Leesburg. Let every voice in the South give its tribute of praise to the determined pluck of the Virginians and Mississippians, who, with a brave leader and against grave odds, drove the Lincolnites before them into the Potomac. The able combination of the troops, the accuracy of their movements, their reckless dash and courage, show the world that the Southern volunteer, with a leader who does not hesitate to give the command "FORWARD," when the enemy shows himself in front, is a match for any soldier in the world. How the news spread through the army! The printing press was superseded that day. If a telegraph line had been working it would have been too slow . . . Reserve supplies of 'army lightning,' . . . were brought to light, and The health of the Palmetto general drank with all the honors . . . . A party of the ¾ Regiment, at dinner, have just come to the deliberate conclusion, that 'one full regiment from each State should be sent up to 'Shanks Evans,' with orders to take Washington,' and they are willing to go their pile on the winnings . . .[42]

The Southern press, while praising Evans, nevertheless was full of rumors that he would be court-martialed for having fought the Federals at Leesburg. Some Southern graduates of West Point did not approve of Evans's judgement at Leesburg. In fact, J. B. Jones, the Confederate war clerk, wrote in his diary on October 23:

The president is highly delighted at the result of the battle of Leesburg; and yet some of the red-tape West Point gentry are indignant at Gen. Evans for not obeying orders and falling back. There is some talk of a court-martial; for it is maintained that no commander, according to strict military rules, should have offered battle against such superior numbers. They may disgrace Gen. Evans; but I trust our *soldiers* will repeat the experiment on every similar occasion.[43]

Evans was not court-martialed. Instead, he received the thanks of the Confederate Congress and the Mississippi Legislature, and his native state voted him a medal. This gave Evans the distinction of being the only officer in the Confederate army who was thus honored for his services by his native state in both the Confederate and United States Army. These honors were gratifying to Evans, but what was more so was the fact that on October 21, 1861, he was commissioned brigadier-general in the Provisional Army of the Confederacy.[44]

Yet another congratulatory letter arrived. But this time it was also a letter of caution as his brother-in-law Mart Gary wrote:

> Allow me to congratulate you on your brilliant victory. I was at Centreville when I heard of it, and I assure you it made my bosom swell with pride and gratification at your splendid success. Everyone spoke of you in the highest terms of praise. You must keep cool and not let success carry you too far. I insist that you will not expose yourself in any future fight, for you are now considered brave to a fault. I heard that Sister Vic was in Richmond. I suppose she is now with you . . . .[45]

Mrs. Evans had been at Leesburg for several days. She was present during the battle and assisted with the wounded and dying, carrying water and doing everything she could to ease their suffering. Mart Gary was very complimentary to Evans in a letter he wrote to his mother on October 30, 1861: "I suppose you have seen that Genl. Evans has distinguished himself having gained one of the most splendid victories that has yet been achieved by our arms. He takes position now with the best Gen'ls of the world."[46]

On October 22, 1861, the Department of Northern Virginia was established with Joseph E. Johnston as its commander. The department was divided into three districts. General Beauregard was assigned to the command of the Potomac District which embraced the territory between the left bank of Powell's River and the Blue Ridge Mountains. Brigadier-General Evans was to be in command of the 4th Brigade of the 4th Division of this District. His brigade was to consist of five North Carolina regiments. The transfer of the various commands was to be made when General Johnston thought it would be most convenient.[47]

Therefore Evans remained stationed at Leesburg with his 7th Brigade. On October 30, Beauregard sent Evans orders to watch Banks's movement across the Potomac, and, if he made a movement eastward, to attempt to check the forces sent out against him. Beauregard advised Evans to fall back toward Manassas by Carter's Mill and Sudley Springs if he was attacked by a superior force.[48]

On November 2, Evans was ordered to turn over the 7th Brigade to Brigadier-General Charles Clark and to report in person at Johnston's headquarters. A week later Brigadier-General Richard Griffin was placed in command of the Mississippi regiments in Loudoun County. He was ordered to report to General Evans, who was in command of all forces in that county. The army headquarters continued to shift the regiments from the different brigades. The newest assignment gave Evans four Georgia regiments.[49] He continued to remain in Leesburg, however, with his same command. He wrote Beauregard on November 18 for instructions. On the following day, Beauregard replied that his instructions were the same as those given on October 30.[50]

Although Evans was fully occupied watching Banks's movements, he was nevertheless thinking of South Carolina. The Federal forces were now menacing the South Carolina coast. Upon hearing of this, Evans asked the Confederate authorities in Richmond to send him to South Carolina that he might help protect his native state from invasion. Officials in South Carolina also wanted him to come. On November 24, Governor F. W. Pickens wrote President Davis that he was well pleased with General R. E. Lee, but that if Lee "had more men like General Evans to make guerilla dashes, it might be a great service to him, particularly if the enemy land large forces on our coast with a view of permanent interior invasion." On November 29, Davis wrote to Pickens that Evans would be sent immediately.[51]

When the 17th Mississippi heard that Evans was leaving, the commissioned officers held a meeting at which they unanimously passed a resolution requesting Evans to present the "battle flag" to the regiment before he left. The following letter was also written on that day:

> The officers and soldiers of the 17th Regiment of Mississippi Volunteers, comprising a part of the brigade under your command, having heard with regret that you have received orders to report for duty at another point have requested the undersigned to convey to you some expression of the feelings to which this intelligence has given rise.
>
> It is now more than four months since you assumed the command of this brigade at the 'Stone Bridge' within sight of a spot rendered memorable by your valor – and since that time we have been constantly in the advance of our line of operations, in the very face of our enemy greatly superior to us in numbers and arms, exposed to all the trials and hardships incident to an active campaign, and to the perils of the bloody but glorious struggle of the 21st of October upon the banks of the Potomac.
>
> During the whole of this time we have ever found you active – vigilant & prudent, guarding every avenue of attack & retreat – and ready to meet the enemy in whatever force they might advance – possessing not only the courage and skill which distinguish the true soldier and the able general, but also those generous impulses as a man which have never failed to make you mindful of the toils & sufferings of the humblest private in the ranks, & ready to use every exertion to lighten his labors & to promote his comfort. And above all you have in you a remarkable degree that wonderful faculty of inspiring all those under your command with that feeling of reliance in you & in themselves which knits the leader & his men 'with hooks of steel' and makes them invincible.
>
> We would fail to do justice to the feelings of those whom we represent, if we did not attempt to express our regret at this sep-

aration – and to tender to you our most cordial wishes for your success in every field of action to which you may be called.[52]

Shortly after his arrival in South Carolina, Evans's official report of the battle of Leesburg was published. Within several months, however, there was some disagreement in the Confederate Congress about the publication of conflicting reports of other Confederate officers who participated in that battle. To resolve the contradictions, on February 26, 1862, the Confederate House of Representatives passed a resolution that called for the report of Colonel Walter Jenifer.[53]

After reading about the passage of the resolution in the newspapers, Evans wrote the secretary of war on March 7 that since Jenifer's report had been called for, he would like to note for the record that there were a number of contradictory statements in the report. Evans added that if reference were made to the reports of the other colonels, a true history of the battle would be ascertained. He concluded by requesting that if Jenifer's report was published, he would like his statement to be published also. After some discussion, it was decided that Evans might make a supplementary report if Beauregard would endorse it, which Beauregard did on April 12.[54]

In the meantime, Evans had written to his friend, Senator Albert Gallatin Brown of Mississippi, concerning the controversy. On April 4, Brown wrote a lengthy, insightful reply that bears repeating:

> Your letter of March 7 was read. In due season and a few days ago that of the 25th came to hand. Both would have been replied to before this but for reasons which I now give. On the receipt of yours on 7th March I made enquiry at once as to who it was that had called for Col. Jenifer's report, and ascertained that the Resolution had been moved on the House of Rept. by Mr. Jenkins of Virginia at the instance of Col. Jenifer himself. I at once handed your letter to Capt. Singleton late of the 18th Miss. And now a member of the House with a request that he move a resolution at once calling for the Reports of Coln'l Hunton, Featherston, & Griffin. He did so promptly. The Sec. of War

Randolph replied within the last few days that his predecessor Benjamin had informed him the *Copies* of these reports had been sent to the Provisional Congress. On calling for these copies they could not be found. I went at once to Mr. Jenkins to know of him if he designed asking for the publication of Col. Jenifer's report and explained to him how it was. That injustice would be done to the other Regiments of the 7th Brigade if that report went to the country unaccompanied with the report of the other Colonels. He said promptly and with the frankness of a true Gentleman that he would not ask the publication of Jenifer's report unless requested to do so by the Col. himself and in that case he would notify Capt. Singleton and myself that he was about to make the motion.

To avoid any possibility of a slip I moved and had passed in the Senate a Resolution calling for the Reports of all the Colonels including Jenifer's. As yet the Sec. has not replied. I mean if one of them is given to the public all shall go. It is a little strange as you will no doubt remark that Sec. Benjamin promptly on call sent Jenifer's report and when the others were called for made an evasive reply through his successor Randolph. There is something wrong and I mean to ferrit it out. The Ex Secr. Curt reply to your note of March 7 (to him) taken in connection with his avoidance of Singleton's resolution shows that he is indisposed to let all the facts be known . . . . I am greatly obliged to you for the jealous care you have shown for the rights and honors of the Mississippians who fought under you at Leesburg and to my own. I am sure that I may add the thanks of all the officers & men of the three Regiments.[55]

Brown's motion was the last reference made to the publication of Jenifer's report, and Evans, seemingly content with the results, moved on to other concerns.

— Chapter VI —

ADAMS' RUN

On December 18, Evans reported for duty at Coosawatchie, South Carolina. The same day, General Robert E. Lee, the commander of the Department of South Carolina and Georgia, assigned Evans to the command of the Third Military District of South Carolina. This district included the territory between the Stono and Ashepoo Rivers, with Evans's headquarters at Adams' Run. Lee quickly assigned Evans a body of troops that had just been mustered into the Confederate service. They were Colonel C. J. Elford's 16th South Carolina Volunteers, Colonel John H. Means's 17th South Carolina Volunteers, and Major G. S. James Laurens's Battalion.[1]

Three days later, Lee ordered Brigadier-General Roswell S. Ripley to leave the troops of his command in the Third Military District until Evans's forces reported. He also instructed Ripley to reinforce Evans if an attack was made on John's Island.

That day, Evans wrote to his wife, who had returned to Cokesbury, about the reception that he had received at this new post: "I have been received with great enthusiasm by my troops and all the ladies wish I were single I have already two sweethearts very sweet." He then told of a letter that he had received from Mart Gary, who was in Virginia: "The people are begging him for my likeness and wishing me to have one taken in full uniform and sent to him as he deems it a part of the history of the war, as I am the only General to who[m] Congress has voted their thanks."[2]

Former Governor William H. Gist expressed the feeling of many South Carolinians when he wrote to Evans: "The people of S. C. are delighted to know, that you have returned to lead them. It did not require the brilliant career you have won in Virginia to satisfy them that, you would nobly do or die in defence of our rights; & what you did, honorable as it was to yourself & useful to your country was nothing more than your state expected."[3]

The Federals made several demonstrations against different points in Evans's district during December and January, but did not attempt an invasion. Evans, nevertheless, kept in constant touch with Lee concerning these raids. In the latter part of December, Evans was deeply concerned over the small number of troops that he had to protect his district and kept asking for reinforcements.[4]

Although busily engaged with his military duties, Evans was also thinking of his family's welfare. On January 17, 1862, he wrote to his wife:

> With reference to the money I wish you to keep every dollar as I am now bargaining for a family of negroes which I can get cheap for cash and send them up the country . . . . I think now is the time to invest what little money we have in negroes. At the end of this month I will have Five Hundred dollars more. So now my dear keep the money subject to my call. I know you are *too economical* don't deprive yourself of any convenience or luxury as I am only actuated by . . . interest for yourself and our darling boy.[5]

At this time the slaves on Edisto Island were causing the Confederates a great deal of trouble. On January 20, an armed body of slaves fired on the Confederate pickets that had been stationed there. Evans acted at once. On January 21, he ordered Colonel P. F. Stevens to proceed the following day with one hundred infantry and a company of cavalry and put down the uprising. Stevens was also instructed to destroy all supplies on Edisto. Stevens left early on the twenty-second and returned on the twenty-fifth, having captured some eighty Black men, women, and children. He also reported that he had destroyed most of the provisions on the island. Evans wrote to Lee that the slaves evidently had been incited to insurrection by the Federals, and he recommended that they be severely punished.[6]

In a letter to his wife in early February, Evans mentioned the Black question: "We have captured nearly a hundred negroes and I have sent the guilty heavily ironed to jail the rest I have employed on the field works, digging intrenchments. I am afraid that negroes up the country have been tampered with also. Some secret individual may be in the vicinity inciting the negroes to insurrection. Tell Frank to stir up his home guard."[7]

On February 12, after several months of demonstrations, the Federals landed a force on Edisto Island. Colonel Henry Moore reported to Washington that if he could be sent ten thousand additional troops, he would be in Charleston in three days. The Federals advanced and drove Evans's pickets from Jehossee Island until they were in striking distance of Adams' Run. Evans informed Lee who, on February 14, ordered Ripley and S. R. Gist to send four companies of infantry and a new regiment, respectively, to Evans's aid immediately.[8]

The following day, Evans alerted Lee that the Federals had occupied Edisto in force and that their pickets had advanced as far as Jehossee. Evans said that he had only 1,305 effective troops and could not strengthen his position in front of Jehossee without weakening the forces on John's and Wadmalaw Islands. He feared that if the Federals occupied Jehossee in large numbers, they could, with the assistance of gunboats and batteries, drive back his small force and cut the Savannah and Charleston Railroad.[9] On the same day, Lee replied that the Confederates did not have enough troops to patrol the whole coast and all that could be done was to find the point of attack and concentrate the Confederate forces at that position.[10]

In the meantime, Evans had sent a recruiting officer to Charleston in an attempt to enlist more men. The Charleston *Daily Courier* urged the Charlestonians to enlist in the infantry, which was the part of Evans's brigade that needed strengthening. The papers further declared that "If Charlestonians would save the city from assault, or defend it successfully, if assaulted, let them rally at once, under the gallant Evans, the laurelled hero of Leesburg."[11]

On February 18, Ripley notified Lee that Evans had only fifteen hundred effectives and that Ripley himself had only fifteen hundred movable troops, which was not enough to make a successful stand. Ripley pointed out to Lee that North Edisto afforded a safe harbor for very large vessels and that from there the Federals could move in force on White Point or Simon's Landing, which was only five to eight miles from the Charleston and Savannah Railroad. He stated further that if the Federals should overcome Evans and cut the railroad and then take Charleston or Savannah, the Confederates would be forced to retire to the interior or live in the unhealthy swamps.[12]

Two days later, Lee informed General John C. Pemberton that Evans and Ripley thought the Federals would advance by White Point and Simon's Landing; if they did, Pemberton was to execute a flanking movement and intercept them.[13]

Evans appeared both gloomy and determined when he wrote home on February 20:

> The gloomy news from Tenn. has cast a gloom over every countenance but I am more determined than ever to fight them to the last extremity, and to die or be free. I am daily expecting an attack in the direction of John's Island and am now making arrangements to meet the enemy. I think he will attack Charleston this week. A simultaneous attack will probably be made on Savannah and Charleston.[14]

In a letter a few days later, Evans was even more pessimistic:

> Gen. Lee telegraphed me yesterday that the enemy had left Savannah probably for my district. Gen. Pemberton came up last night to consult how he could best support me. So if the Yankees should attack me I will be well supported. . . .Vic you do not say how you are. Sometimes I think I will never see you again & often do I find myself thinking of such a probability. There is now no prospect of our meeting soon as you cannot come to see me

and I cannot by any means leave my district. So let us cheer each other that a Kind Providence may yet permit us to meet again.[15]

The Federals did not advance, which was fortunate for Evans, who was confined to his room with influenza for a large part of the time. On March 2, he wrote his wife that he was feeling much better and had sent her some money. Still interested in buying slaves, he urged economy. As usual, he ended his letter by saying:

> I feel if I could only see you and our *ugly* boy *one hour* I would get well. You must pinch him hard everyday for his father and tell him when I come I will give him a hundred . . . When you write your letters do them in the daytime. Do for my sake. Don't expose your eyes as you know how I love them.[16]

As devoted to his wife's family as he was his own, Evans wrote her on March 8:

> I do not wish mother to take any boarders whatever . . . The great affection for yourself and myself would prompt me to undergo any deprivation for her comfort. So you must not let Mother want for *anything* whatever. . . .Vic it is your Christian duty to look out for Mother's wants, if she does not tell you find out and write me what she wants. In these times of war we must make arrangements far ahead as everything will be much higher and money more scarce. . . . Come to Charleston and buy now what you will want for the next two years. This will be economy as well as a comfort.[17]

On March 2, Lee received a dispatch from Davis urging him to report to Richmond as soon as possible. About two weeks later, Pemberton was notified that Lee had been retained in Richmond and that he was to assume command of the Department of South Carolina and Georgia.[18]

Although the Federals had not attempted an invasion of the mainland in Evans's district, they were still sending reconnoitering parties. Evans tells of capturing several men in a March 18 letter to his wife:

My pickets succeeded yesterday in capturing three Yankees
. . . They (although armed) made no resistance to my guard of
three men. I have sent them to Charleston . . . . I am now prepar-
ing to attack them on the Island. I think I have them a little frightened. I went down yesterday and opened fire on them from the
Pineberry Battery. Crossed over four companies but enemy
retired. I think he will make a feint to recover his prisoners. I am
prepared with a force of 5000 to meet him and feel well assured
should he come on the mainland I can whip him.[19]

On March 21, Evans visited the Camp of Instruction, located in
St. Andrew's Parish. After the troops were reviewed, Captain Asa
Lewis Evans, his brother and aide, presented a sword captured at
Leesburg to the Evans Guard, which was named in honor of the
general. Captain W. J. Gooding received the sword and pledged
that his company would prove worthy of the name they had cho-
sen. The sword bore the inscription: "Capt. Pierson, Twentieth
Massachusetts Volunteers," above which had been added by
Evans, "Presented to the Evans Guard by Brigadier-General N. G.
Evans, March 22d, 1862. Captured at the battle of Leesburg, Va.,
October 21, 1861." [20] Five days later, Evans wrote his wife:

Vic I am always afraid for you to come for they have measles
among the children. I am very anxious to see you and the baby
as I think I will be ordered either to Virginia or to the West in May
and probably will not be able to see you again for some time, so
you can imagine my feelings. I do not think the enemy will attack
us this spring as the sickly season is fast approaching and they
cannot live in these swamps. . . .The enemy are very quiet con-
fining themselves to Edisto Island and their Gunboats.[21]

Around the middle of March, Evans received information that
the Federals had advanced from Edisto Island to Little Edisto Island
with the intention of crossing to the mainland at Edisto Ferry or
Pineberry. Evans dispatched a scouting party, which reported that
the Federals had stationed four companies on the northern extremity of both islands. Colonel P. F. Stevens of the Holcombe Legion
confirmed this report. Therefore, Evans decided to attack the

Federals. He appointed Stevens as the commander of the expedition and told him to make the proper arrangements.

About 3:00 A.M. on March 29, Stevens, with the Holcombe Legion, the Enfield Battalion, and a detachment of dismounted cavalry, crossed at Watt's Cut. After advancing for some distance to the Old Dominion house, the detachment split up according to Evans's orders. Major F. G. Palmer, with some 260 men, turned to the left and moved toward the bridge to Little Edisto Island. After driving the Federal pickets from the bridge, Palmer's command crossed and burned the bridge. He then proceeded to round up the trapped Federal troops on the island. He succeeded in capturing twenty-one prisoners but the rest escaped in a dense fog. Stevens advanced on Edisto and drove the Federals back to their artillery. He then sent to Evans for instructions. Evans, who had crossed the Edisto River at sunrise and was stationed on Jehossee, thought that the enemy was in too large a force for Stevens to attack so he ordered him to retreat. The troops of both commands were back at Pineberry by 11 A.M. Two Federals were killed in the affair and a number wounded, while the Confederates had several slightly wounded.[22]

On April 3, one of the members of the staff of the Charleston *Daily Courier*, accompanied by "Personne" and a nurse, visited Adams' Run. The purpose of their trip was to visit the hospitals and to bring money and supplies. There were five hospitals, all of which were located in large homes. The hospitals were under the care of Dr. F. M. Geddings, with Dr. James Evans, the general's brother, and Dr. Lingard Frampton, as assistants. After describing the hospitals, the correspondent stated that General Evans "is fully sensible that he holds the key to Charleston and will do *tout son possible* to strengthen his position, and make of Adams' Run another Thermopolas, himself being its Leonidas before Charleston shall be taken or invested by land."[23]

The following day, the correspondent wrote an account of the part the Evans family was taking in the war. Besides the general, there were five brothers who were in active service. Lieutenant Beverly Daniel Evans was serving in Stonewall Jackson's brigade, while Alfred and James Evans were surgeons with an Alabama regiment and at Adams' Run, respectively. Asa Lewis Evans was assistant adjutant-general at Adams' Run, while Lieutenant William Edwin Evans was serving on the Confederate war steamer *Sumter*. The correspondent also listed Chesley Daniel Evans, Andrew Jackson Evans, and Thomas Evans, and also Sarah Jane Singletary, whose husband, Captain Robert L. Singletary, was a captain in the 8th Regiment of South Carolina Volunteers. The article ended with the recommendation "that such a family group of Confederate warriors deserve the 'well done' of their country, and ought to be daguerreotyped or photographed, in one picture, for the admiration of the present and future generations of patriot Southerners."[24]

About this time, Evans received an answer to a letter written to Lee in reference to the promotion of Colonel Richard DeTreville. Lee replied:

> I have recd. your letter of 21st & conversed with the President in reference to Col. De Treville & communicated your opinion of that officer. I am glad to find that he stands so high in your estimation for I was much pleased with him.
>
> You are aware that Genl. Gist has been appd. Br. Genl. from S.C. & I do not think that another appt. from that State is contemplated at present.
>
> Wishing you health and happiness & that you may drive our enemies who are pressing us so hard everywhere out of your State at least.[25]

There was some dissatisfaction over the appointment of Gist, and Evans wrote to Lee concerning this. In replying Lee said:

> I regret to learn by your letter of the 7th that the appointment of Genl. Gist has given dissatisfaction to the good people of S.C. He and Genl. DeSassaure I think were recommended by the authorities & he was selected, only one Brigr. being supposed necessary at the time. From what I saw of Genl. Gist I was much pleased with him. He exhibited intelligence & energy & moreover showed devotion to the Service. I hope Cols. Jones and Dunnovant will not resign. No one ought to take exception at the promotion of others when made in conformity to laws or consid-

er it a reflection upon themselves. It cannot be supposed that the Pres. Can know & weigh the qualifications & claims of every citizen and soldier, nor is it possible for him in every instance to select the best man for office. He has to exercise his best judgment upon the knowledge & information before him & must in the nature of things make mistakes. It is not intentional on his part & the loss is the Countrys. Those that feel that they have the ability & are better qualified than those selected, ought to endeavor by increased diligence & zeal to make good the loss thus sustained by the Country. There is no struggle for individual profit or advancement & I am convenced everyone feels it so, & is willing to take any position where he can be useful.

I am much gratified at your success in driving the enemy at Edisto. Keep at them my dear Genl. & give them no rest or peace. They are pressing us everywhere & it requires our renewed & united efforts to keep them at bay. I have great reliance upon you and the Army in S.C.[26]

General David Hunter, who succeeded General Thomas W. Sherman in command of the Federal troops in the Department of the South on March 31, 1862, reported that there were fourteen hundred troops on Edisto Island. These troops were a constant menace to Evans since, with the aid of gunboats, they made frequent demonstrations in the Third Military District. On April 29, the Federals completed a typical reconnaissance. They came up the Dawdo in the gunboat *Hale* and attacked and destroyed the battery of two 24-pounder guns at Pineberry after an engagement of about four hours. Evans, with two pieces of field artillery, met the Federals near Willstown. The enemy retired to the gunboat, but Evans, by watching their movements closely, engaged the Federals again near White Point. After exchanging fire for nearly an hour, the Federals retreated. The casualties were slight on both sides.[27]

Evans's wife arrived at Adams's Run in April and stayed some time with her husband, leaving around the middle of May. Evans was busily engaged in helping prepare a defense for a Federal invasion that was growing more ominous. On May 25, Evans proceeded to John's Island with eight companies of infantry, only to find that the Federals had departed. He rounded up some two hundred slaves, whom he sent to Charleston to be claimed by their owners.[28]

The Federals continued to make attacks upon the different Confederate batteries along the shore. They grew bolder in the latter part of May, and an invasion of Charleston seemed imminent. An event occurred on May 13 which no doubt gave impetus to the Federal invasion. On this day, the abduction of the Confederate Steamer *Planter* by some of the slaves working onboard caused a great sensation in Charleston. The vessel escaped to the Federal lines, and the crew reported to the Federals that the guns had been removed from the Georgetown defenses and at Cole's Island, which was situated at the mouth of the Stono River.[29]

Pemberton had formed his new line south of Charleston along the Savannah and Charleston Railroad. He had drawn in his defense on James Island to Secessionville, on the east side of the island to Fort Pemberton on the Stono.[30] Pemberton was severely criticized by Governor Pickens and a great number of military men, as well as the citizens of Charleston. Ripley requested to be relieved of his post and was ordered to Richmond on May 26. Brigadier-General H. W. Mercer assumed command of the Second Military District of South Carolina. Two days later, Pemberton organized the Department of South Carolina into divisions and brigades. Evans was assigned to the command of the Second Military District of South Carolina of the 1st Division, while Mercer received command of the First Military District of the same division.[31]

The Federals, under the command of General H. W. Benham, landed troops on Battery Island on June 2, and by June 5, a large force was stationed on James Island. Benham's line extended opposite Secessionville on his right to the Stono on his left. During the next ten days there were several minor engagements between the opposing troops with a few casualties on both sides.

On June 15, Pemberton assigned Evans to the command of the First Military District. That afternoon, Evans was notified by Colonel T. G. Lamar, who was stationed at Secessionville, that he would probably be attacked that night or the following morning. Evans directed Lamar to hold his position and promised that he would reinforce him if necessary. Early the next morning, Lamar notified Evans that the Federals were advancing. Evans went immediately to the Clark house, where he arrived at 4:15 A.M. There he found Colonel Johnson Hagood, who had three regiments in readiness for an immediate attack. Hagood already had sent a detachment to support Lamar. Evans then sent Colonel S. D. Goodlet's regiment and the 4th Louisiana Battalion to Secessionville. These forces arrived in time to assist in repulsing the second Federal charge at Secessionville. At this time, the Federals were advancing on Evans's right, so he ordered Hagood to attack them and sent the 51st Georgia Regiment and Colonel Williams's regiment to Hagood's support. The conflict now became general on both ends of the line. Finally at about 10:00 A.M., the Federals retreated, leaving many dead and wounded upon the field.[32]

The Confederates lost 52 killed, 144 wounded, and 8 captured or missing, while the Federals sustained 107 killed, 487 wounded, and 89 captured or missing. Forty-three of the Federals who were classed as wounded were captured by the Confederates.[33]

With the repulse at Secessionville, the Federals appeared convinced that the line across James Island was too strong to penetrate, so in late June they evacuated James Island and moved their troops to North Edisto, Hilton Head, and Beaufort.[34]

On July 13, General Samuel Cooper notified Pemberton that the Confederates needed reinforcements at Richmond immediately and that President Davis desired as many troops as Pemberton could spare. Cooper stated further that the president thought that since it was the season for much sickness on the coast, Pemberton could send him more than half of his effective force. Pemberton was instructed to place Brigadier-Generals Evans and T. F. Drayton in charge of the troops.[35]

Two days later, Evans received orders to proceed at once to Richmond in command of Means's 17th Regiment South Carolina Volunteers, H. L. Benbow's 23rd Regiment South Carolina Volunteers, J. M. Gadberry's 18th Regiment South Carolina Volunteers, and the Holcombe Legion. His artillery consisted of W. D. Leake's Virginia Battery and R. Boyce's South Carolina Battery. More excitement was thus to come for Evans and his command.[36]

— *Chapter VII* —

SECOND
MANASSAS AND
ANTIETAM

A fter the battle of Malvern Hill in early July, McClellan had withdrawn his forces to Harrison Landing on the James River. In the meantime, Major-General John Pope had been called from the West and placed in command of the Army of Virginia. Pope's troops were stationed near Alexandria and were moving toward Richmond by the Orange and Alexandria Railroad.

On July 12, news of the Federal occupation of Culpeper Courthouse reached Lee. The next day, he ordered Jackson with his and Ewell's Division to proceed, if possible, to Gordonsville to defend the line of the Virginia Central Railroad which connected Richmond with the Shenandoah Valley. Lee, on July 27, realizing that Jackson was greatly outnumbered, ordered A. P. Hill's division and the Louisiana brigade to join Jackson at Gordonsville. The Confederates were faced with meeting two strong armies in different directions.

This was the situation facing Evans and his South Carolina brigades when they reached Richmond. On July 28, Lee ordered them to report to Longstreet "to be encamped and kept together for the present as a distinct organization." Soon after his arrival, Evans wrote to his wife:

> I have been temporarily assigned to Genl. Longstreet's Division but expect to have a Division of my own before long . . . . I called this morning on Genl. Lee and found him in excellent spirits. He was delighted to see me and asked particularly for you to know why I did not bring you with me. I answered that everything was so high I could not afford it. The Army as far as I have seen are in fine spirits and ready for another fight. Genl. Lee however does not expect another fight near this place, but is determined to drive the Vandal, Pope out of the valley of Virginia. Pope I think can be easily driven back. I have met a number of friends and old acquaintances since my arrival who have universally congratulated me on the James Island affair. It seems in spite of Pemberton's refusal to report my presence on the Island Genl. Cooper has given me due credit and Genl. Lee says I saved Charleston. My old brigade the Mississippians flocked to greet me and begged me to come back to them. That nobody but myself knew how to command them. I do wish I had them as I know they *will* fight. I have applied for them . . . .[1]

Three days later Evans again apprised his wife of the situation:

> The enemy is leaving his position on James River and I feel convinced we will not have another fight near Richmond, and not for some days in the valley of Virginia. The enemy has been reinforcing Genl. Pope for several days, and I am expecting a fight with Jackson's forces every day, and should it please God to give us another victory in the Valley I think the war in Virginia will stop for awhile. I will move into camp tomorrow. Col. Means marched his Regiment through town today and halted in front of the hotel to offer me a salute which I declined. I have met several of my Leesburg lady friends. . .Genl. Lee has promised me to send me up into that country should the occasion occur. I think the enemy has become convinced that he cannot take our capitol with his present army . . . .[2]

It soon appeared that Lee and Evans were mistaken about McClellan's intentions. On August 5, Lee was notified that

McClellan had advanced from Westover to Malvern Hill and was again threatening Richmond. The following day, Lee ordered Longstreet's, Ripley's, and Lafayette McLaws's divisions to advance toward Malvern Hill. It was about sunset when the Confederates drew up in line of battle. Evans's brigade formed a part of Longstreet's division, which was stationed on the Confederate right. Lee instructed Evans's and Howell Cobb's brigades to move upon Malvern Hill. Evans advanced through a body of woods, arriving at a wheat field on the opposite side. The Confederates continued their march through the wheat, where they observed picket stations that had been hastily deserted. Evans halted his brigade shortly after dark. A little later, a Federal cavalry detachment appeared on a road where the flank of the 18th South Carolina rested. Evans immediately opened fire and the cavalry hastily retreated. Several of the Federals were killed and four captured. The following morning, the Confederates discovered that McClellan had retreated to Westover during the night.

In reporting the engagement, Lee stated: "The . . . operation was handsomely executed by General Evans with his own and Cobb's brigade, forcing the enemy back to his guns on Malvern Hill." Several days later Evans himself wrote to his wife:

> Today I received orders to go to Gordonsville to reinforce Jackson and will leave probably tomorrow tho' I am scarcely able. I have had an attack of dysentery for the last three days and am now much debillitated. I will however go cheerfully. The forces of the enemy have retired from this vicinity and have evidently gone to reinforce Pope. We are making great preparations to attack the enemy in the valley but I think as soon as we concentrate our forces the enemy will *"skedoodle."*[3]

On August 13, Lee obtained information that both Burnside and McClellan were withdrawing from the peninsula in order to reinforce Pope. Lee decided to attack Pope before the Federal reinforcements could reach him. Leaving D. H. Hill's and McLaws's divisions to watch McClellan, he ordered Longstreet's command, which included Evans's brigade, to proceed at once by the Virginia Central Railroad to Gordonsville.[4]

On August 15, Lee decided, after a conference with his generals, to strike Pope at Culpeper Courthouse. Fitzhugh Lee's cavalry, however, were a day late in arriving; as a result, the attack was postponed until the twentieth. In the meantime, Pope, learning that Lee had reinforced Jackson, retreated immediately and took his position on the eastern bank of the Rappahannock River.

Lee attempted to effect a crossing up the Rappahannock but Pope followed him up the other bank. On the twenty-third, when the left wing of the Confederate army marched from Rappahannock station, the Federals sent a large force to the west bank and supported it with well-mounted artillery. Longstreet ordered Evans with his brigade to support the batteries of Major John J. Garnett which were attacking the Federals at this point. The brigade moved against the Federals, who retreated across the bridge at their approach. Upon gaining the opposite side of the bridge, the Federals set fire to it. The Confederates held the position they had taken but suffered severely from the fire of the Northern batteries. Evans ordered Captain Boyce to mount his battery on a steep hill, but upon reaching the top, Boyce was forced to retire because of the severe shelling of the Federal batteries. Evans had twenty-seven men killed and eighty-four wounded in this engagement.[5]

On the night of the twenty-second, Stuart's Cavalry had attacked Catlett Station and captured several members of Pope's staff. Of more importance to the Confederates, he brought back Pope's dispatch book. From this Lee learned that Pope had 45,000 men and was expecting Burnside and McClellan to join him. Lee decided to maneuver Pope away from McClellan and cut his supply lines from Washington. At a conference with Jackson on the twenty-fourth, it was decided that Jackson with three divisions was to cross the Rappahannock at Waterloo Bridge and proceed to Pope's rear, cutting Pope's line of communications with the capital.

Jackson left early the next morning, Longstreet replacing him at Waterloo Bridge. Jackson made a long, circuitous, fifty-four-mile march in two days, encamping at Bristoe Station behind Pope on the evening of the twenty-seventh. A little later that evening Stuart took the Federal supply depot at Manassas Junction. On the following day, Lee moved with Longstreet's command towards Thoroughfare Gap to join Jackson. They passed through Thoroughfare Gap on the night of the twenty-ninth, after being held for some time by the Federals.

In the interim, Jackson had become engaged, withdrawing to a long ridge near Grovetown. On the morning of the twenty-ninth, he discovered that the Federals were farther to his left. For this reason he changed his position, forming along a cut of the "unfinished railroad" of the Manassas Gap line to Alexandria. He expected Longstreet to join him on the right of this line.

At 9 A.M. Longstreet passed through Gainesville. Upon hearing the sounds of the battle in the distance, the Confederates marched faster and arrived some thirty minutes later at the scene of hostilities. John B. Hood's brigades, supported by Evans's brigade, were stationed across the turnpike. Cadmus M. Wilcox's three brigades supported Hood's and Evans's rear. The Washington Artillery was placed between Hood's left and Jackson's right. About noon Longstreet had formed his line for battle.

In the meantime, Jackson was heavily engaged and had thrown back charge after charge of the Federals. Pope, unaware of Lee's and Longstreet's presence and anxious to overwhelm Jackson, wanted General Fitz-John Porter to advance through the woods on Stuart's hill so that Jackson's right would be crushed. Porter, suspecting that Longstreet was there, refused to move his ten thousand men through the woods until he was sure that they were not too heavily occupied by the Confederates. On the other hand, Lee could not persuade Longstreet to advance. After being urged to advance three times, Longstreet finally agreed that it would be a good idea to move under the cover of darkness to get the troops in a favorable position for an attack the next morning. As it happened, the Federals advanced at the same time, and an engagement took place between the Federal left and Hood's brigades strongly supported by Evans.

These brigades, supported by those of Wilcox, drove the enemy from their positions. As the Federals fell back, darkness concealed their movements; so Evans drew up his brigade in the retreating troops' former camp. Later, Evans, having been ordered to withdraw by Longstreet, fell back about a mile leaving a strong picket to guard his front.[6]

On the morning of the thirtieth, the Confederate line of battle remained the same as it had been on the previous day. Jackson still maintained his position along the "unfinished railroad," while Colonel S. D. Lee's batteries were on his left, with Longstreet in the woods on Stuart's hill to the right of the batteries.

Pope, still thinking that Jackson had not been reinforced, decided to launch another attack against him. A little after the middle of the day, his troops advanced against Jackson and met with terrific resistance. The Federal onslaught continued until about four o'clock in the afternoon, when Lee ordered an advance all along the Confederate line.

Earlier in the day, Evans had been placed in command of Hood's two brigades, George E. Pickett's brigade under Hunton, and his own. But before the orders to advance arrived, Hunton was ordered to James L. Kemper's support. When the orders to advance came, Evans's division moved forward and soon was hotly engaged. Although losing men heavily, the men advanced on with the rest of the Confederate line.[7]

The advance of Lee's whole army proved to be too much for the Federals. The Confederate line, four miles long, pushed on with each division formed in at least two lines. In the center of the line where Kemper and R. H. Anderson supported Evans, there were eight brigades. The Confederates continued to advance until they drove the Federals back to Henry Hill, where they held until darkness ended the fighting. During the night, Pope retired to the fortifications of Centreville, some four miles distant.

On the thirty-first, Lee ordered Jackson to turn Pope's right at Centreville. Jackson moved at once, but this time Pope had been informed of the movement and retreated to Fairfax Court House. After an engagement with Jackson on September 2, at Chantilly, Pope retreated to the fortifications of Alexandria and Washington. On the same day McClellan assumed command of the Federal army.

The Confederates won a great victory at Second Manassas, but several brigades suffered heavily. Among those was Evans's brigade, which lost 33 killed, 240 wounded, and 1 missing.[8] Evans lamented the losses in a letter to his wife:

> I have just come through another hard battle. My brigade suffered severely. I lost Col. Means who died blessing me. Col. Gadberry was shot down in the charge. I lost eight captains out of one Regiment. I was under fire the whole time and thank Heaven came out unhurt. Mart was under my command in the thickest of the fight. Billy went as a private in the Holcombe Legion. Had his gun struck three times. . . . We fought on the old field of Manassas. I recognized the place and felt confident we would be successful. . . . The woods in our rear are strewn with the dead Yankees. The stench is awful. The wretches will not send back to bury their dead.[9]

On September 3, Lee issued orders that started the Confederates on their march toward Maryland. Lee realized that the Confederacy had much to gain if they could successfully invade Maryland and the Northern states. If the Southern army was victorious over the Federals on their own soil, it might mean the end of the war and the independence of the Confederacy. Then, too, a great victory following so closely after the rout of Pope would probably mean the intervention of the great European powers. Other reasons for Lee's decision to advance were to replenish his supplies and the hope that, once in Maryland, the Southern sympathizers there would flock to the Confederate ranks.

Although the Confederate soldiers were half starved and half clothed, they were in excellent spirits as they marched along. Evans was also in a good mood as he wrote to his wife from near Leesburg:

> We have but little to eat. My breakfast is generally a roasting ear of corn no meat or coffee. I bought two ducks yesterday and Tom and Romeo [his slaves] are now preparing them for dinner. I am however in good health and spirits and hope to be in Baltimore or Washington in ten days. The enemy has moved all the state papers etc. from Washington. He is evidently much frightened and his army is much cut up and entirely disorganized. We are nearly a hundred thousand strong and flushed with

victory . . . Mart has just come to see me – talkative as ever – says he don't know when he can return says he is going to Maryland. Brags a lot about his legion . . . Will send for you when we get into Washington City.[10]

While on the march to Maryland, Evans placed General Hood under arrest for disobedience of orders. At Manassas, Hood's Texans had captured some ambulances which Hood kept for the use of his brigades. Evans ordered Hood to turn over the ambulances to Evans's South Carolina brigade but Hood refused. Hood contended that since his brigade captured the ambulances they were the rightful owners. As the Confederates were proceeding to Frederick, Maryland, Longstreet ordered Hood to return to Culpeper Courthouse and wait for a court-martial. As soon as Lee heard of the matter, he sent instructions for Hood to remain with his command, but he did not release Hood from arrest.[11]

The Confederates evacuated Frederick on September 10, leaving in different directions. Jackson was sent to capture the Federal garrisons stationed at Martinsburg and Harpers Ferry, while Longstreet moved across South Mountain and up the valley to Hagerstown. By the evening of the thirteenth, the Confederates had crossed South Mountain, leaving a portion of Stuart's Cavalry to guard the gaps.

In the meantime, McClellan had obtained a copy of Lee's orders. But still thinking that Lee greatly outnumbered him, he advanced slowly toward South Mountain. As soon as Lee heard that McClellan was advancing, he sent General D. H. Hill's division that was stationed at Boonesborough to defend the gaps of South Mountain and ordered Longstreet to return from Hagerstown to the support of Hill.

Upon their arrival at South Mountain, Longstreet sent Evans's division to Brigadier-General R. E. Rodes's support on the left of the road near South Mountain. As the troops were marching up the mountain, Longstreet notified Evans that Hood's brigades[12] had been detached to support the Confederate right. Longstreet instructed Evans to hold his position on the left and promised reinforcements. Upon arriving at the top of the mountain, Evans ordered Colonel P. F. Stevens to push over the opposite side in order to give assistance to Rodes. Stevens proceeded with Evans's brigade and soon became engaged. The South Carolinians held their position for some time against superior numbers. But the long march they had made from Hagerstown and the heavy pressure being exerted upon them began to take their toll. They finally broke and retreated to the road. As darkness fell, the Federals did not push their advantage. That night Evans's division acted as rear guard for the army as it retreated to Sharpsburg.[13]

The following morning Hood's brigades were detached from Evans's division, which left Evans with only his and George T. Anderson's brigade. Evans's command was ordered to defend the bridge over the Antietam from Boonesborough and to support Colonel John B. Walton's battery. There was no serious fighting on the fifteenth and sixteenth, though Evans's skirmishers were constantly engaged with the Federal sharpshooters.[14]

On the seventeenth, McClellan decided to attack, but he had given Jackson time to return from Harpers Ferry with all his command except A. P. Hill's division, which was on its way. McClellan sent in his powerful army in piecemeal fashion. In the early part of the battle, he directed divisions and corps across the Antietam through cornfields and woods to attack the Confederate right, but the Federals were repulsed by Jackson, both sides losing heavily. Finally, McClellan attacked Lee's center and left in the same fashion across the Sunken Road on the Confederate left, which received its name of Bloody Lane on this day. Lee met each charge by shifting his forces to the most vulnerable point. In the afternoon, Burnside's corps swept across the Antietam at the stone bridge, but were stoutly met by Robert Toombs, who is better known as an orator than as a general. Toombs's brigade held its position for some time, but was finally swept back to the outskirts of the village. Defeat seemed imminent. Ambrose P. Hill, however, appeared upon the scene with his division. He struck the Federal flank with a terrific charge, and the Federals could not withstand this new thrust and were driven back, losing the ground they had gained. As Burnside's corps retired, the battle of Antietam was virtually ended as night soon enveloped the field.

Evans was stationed where the main road to Boonesborough enters Sharpsburg on the north. In the early part of the battle, his command acted as a reserve for the batteries on both sides of the road. About noon, Evans was ordered to send George T. Anderson's brigade to the support of D. H. Hill. This left Evans with only one brigade — his own — which had been reduced to a mere skeleton because of casualties, sickness, and straggling.[15]

At two o'clock in the afternoon, Evans rallied the troops that had retreated from the Confederate left into Sharpsburg. Aided by his entire staff, Evans finally collected some 250 men, whom he placed under the command of Colonels A. H. Colquitt and Alfred Iverson. Evans sent his command forward to meet the Federal advance. Colquitt and Iverson, with Boyce's battery, met the advance on the right, while Stevens, supported by two batteries of S. D. Lee's battalion, advanced on the left. Stevens pushed forward, but, seeing that he was flanked on both sides, retired behind a stone wall. He soon discovered that he had left Boyce's battery exposed, so he resumed his position at the front. The Federals were finally driven from their cover in the front and were forced to retire. Evans's forces held their positions until night, when he ordered them to return to their original station. There they bivouacked for the night, sleeping on their weapons.[16]

The Confederates prepared to resist another Federal attack the next day. Evans assumed his position in front of the town, acting as the support of the artillery stationed there. His brigade, however, had suffered heavily during the past few days from both casualties and straggling. In fact, Evans reported to Lee on the eighteenth that he had only twelve hundred men present for duty.[17] The Federals did not renew the attack, so that night the battle-worn Confederates retired from Sharpsburg and crossed the Potomac into Virginia.

Reaching Shepherdstown, Virginia, on the nineteenth, Evans wrote his wife:

> We have just fought the great battle a hundred thousand against us. We fought all day under a heavy artillery fire. Our loss is great but not as much as that of the enemy. We retired

across the river last night in good order after resting one day on the battle field. Mart and Billy are safe. I was under fire nearly all day and thank Heaven was spared. My little Secretary Trezevant was shot in the leg immediately in my rear by a shell. His leg was completely taken off .... I am nearly worn out for want of sleep and something to eat .... I have not yet seen my wagons for ten days but sleep pretty comfortably on the ground with my Mexican blanket . . . The Yankees I think feel convinced we can whip them. This battle was the greatest I have been in. All of our forces were engaged in line of battle five miles long.[18]

After arriving in Virginia, Lee let his command recuperate. McClellan assisted him in this by waiting some time to cross the Potomac. Except for the work required in destroying transportation facilities in their front and watching for the enemy, the troops were permitted to rest in peaceful camps.

In one of the camps, Evans was troubled over the problem of how his men could stand the winter. In a letter to his wife at this time he wrote: "We are in good spirits but very tired of war. I have written to Genl. Beauregard if South Carolina is again invaded to apply for My brigade as I know my men will not be able to stand the winter in this climate clothed as they are . . . ."[19]

It appeared that Evans would remain in Virginia, although he still had hopes of returning to South Carolina as he confided to his wife:

> My application to go to South Carolina has been disapproved. Genl. Lee says I am of too much importance to be spared at this time but if any troops should be required in South Carolina he will send me. I think I will return next month. At least I hope so. My Brigade are all anxious to return. . . . Although I expect hard fighting in So. Ca. I would gladly return to spend the winter in a warmer climate. Today it is raining and my men are without tents standing under the trees. The weather has become quite cool. . . .[20]

During this time, Lee exerted his efforts, not only to recruiting new men, but to clothing his troops. In October, the clothes arrived, while diligent efforts on the part of his officers had brought in numerous stragglers. Due to the return of these men and to the recuperation of the wounded, the Army of Northern Virginia increased from fewer than 50,000 men on September 22 to 79,595 on October 20. During this time Evans's brigade increased from 556 men to 1,595.[21]

Evans, still thinking of South Carolina, spoke of the improvements in the army in a letter to Vic: "Our army has recruited a great deal and having received new clothes we feel ready to fight again. I see no prospect of being ordered to South Carolina at least for a month or two. Not until Charleston is attacked, when I hope to go home as it is getting cold here and my men are suffering for the want of blankets. . . ."[22]

On October 27, Lee wrote George W. Randolph, the Confederate secretary of war, that Longstreet's corps was composed of five divisions. Evans's brigade had been assigned to McLaws's division of this corps but Evans was soon sent to North Carolina. On November 6, he was ordered to proceed with his brigade to Weldon, North Carolina, by way of Richmond.[23]

On the same day, he received the following letter from General McLaws:

> Your orders are to report at Genl. Longstreet's Headquarters when you are ready to move and I will go forward at once to receive orders and on my return will notify you. It will be necessary for you to get another day's rations of bacon and the Division Commissary went forward a few minutes since to supply your brigade etc. with it. That will require a little time & it will also be necessary to turn over your wagons; My Division Qr. Master has been ordered to attend to that. You had better send your Brigade Qr. Master to be in readiness to turn over his property.
>
> I am very sorry to lose you and your Brigade from the Army of North Virginia. You have illustrated your State so gloriously and gallantly that while regretting your departure on our account, ending one must rejoice that you have an opportunity of going towards your own State to defend your own homes & firesides & you will carry with you the good will of all and the firm

conviction that wherever you may be, you will always be referred to with pride, as representative of the glory & honor of your Chivalric State.[24]

Evans's brigade arrived in Richmond the following day. Yet the brigade was improperly outfitted for the climate in that section. As they marched by the office of the secretary of war, a large number of the soldiers were plodding through the melting snow barefoot. A bystander counted twenty-five in the final regiment that passed who were without shoes.[25] Evans proceeded from Richmond to assume his new duties in North Carolina.

— *Chapter VIII* —

KINSTON

Soon after reporting to Major-General Gustavus W. Smith in North Carolina, Evans was assigned the command of the troops between the Neuse and Roanoke Rivers. His brigade was stationed at Kinston, North Carolina, on the Neuse River, which is about thirty-five miles from New Bern, where a large Federal force was concentrated. Kinston was located in a strategic position, because of its nearness to the railroad line that connected Virginia with the lower South.[1]

Evans was anticipating hard fighting on all fronts, judging from a letter written to his wife at this time:

> Should the enemy attack Richmond soon I will probably be ordered back to Virginia . . . .The enemy annoy my pickets below here but I do not think however that Foster will come out in two or three weeks not until Richmond is attacked. I am daily expecting to hear of the fight between Lee and Burnside and feel confident we will whip him. The month of December will be a memorable one. Richmond, Weldon, Wilmington, and Charleston are to be attacked with heavy forces and if it should please Heaven to give us the victory I think the war will be over.[2]

For the next few weeks, the Federals remained at New Bern, but continued to engage Evans's pickets. Evans, while watching the

Federal movements, was thinking about the prospects of being promoted to major-general. Indeed, on December 5, he wrote to his wife on this subject:

> I have been in low spirits and pretty well disgusted at my treatment by the authorities in Richmond. The President whilst acknowledging my services has not promoted me, tho' I was, I understand, highly recommended. I think my application to go to So. Ca. has prejudiced all of them against me as the state is not in favor of the Administration. But I console myself that 'Time at length sets all things.' I will bide my time. I am too independent to beg . . . .[3]

In December, the Federals commenced their long-awaited drive towards Richmond. Included in their plan of attack was the cutting of the railroad connections to Richmond, thereby preventing Lee's army in Virginia from receiving much-needed supplies from the lower South. One of these lines passed near Goldsboro, North Carolina. General John G. Foster's command, stationed at New Bern, received the assignment of cutting this line.

On December 11, Foster left New Bern with a large Federal force consisting of about ten thousand infantry, an artillery detachment of forty guns, and a cavalry force of 640 men. After marching fourteen miles down the main Kinston road, Foster's progress was stopped by trees the Confederates had felled across the road for nearly a mile. The Federals halted at this point for the night and removed the obstructions before morning. Foster's march was interrupted when he was engaged by a small Confederate cavalry force under the command of Colonel John A. Baker about twenty miles from Kinston. The Federals surrounded and cut this force to pieces, rendering it practically useless for the remainder of the campaign. On the night of the twelfth, Foster bivouacked about ten miles from Kinston.[4]

Foster's advance took the Confederates completely by surprise. Evans had separated his small command, stationing them at vulnerable points along a thirty-five-mile line. He had stationed the Holcombe Legion and the 18th South Carolina at Greenville some thirty-five miles from Kinston. Their orders were to guard his rear against a possible Federal movement by Washington, North Carolina, where the Union forces were concentrated in considerable force. The Holcombe Legion did not reach Kinston until the night of the thirteenth, while the 18th South Carolina was ordered to remain at Greenville to protect the Confederate rear. Evans, unaware of the Federal advance, was at Greenville inspecting forces. During his absence, Colonel James D. Radcliffe was in command of the Confederates located at Kinston. On the twelfth, Radcliffe formed his line of battle on Southwest Creek, about four miles west of Kinston, after he destroyed the bridge over the creek on the Kinston road. His command consisted of the 17th, 22nd, and 23rd South Carolina Regiments and the 61st Regiment North Carolina State Troops, which was stationed at Hines' Mill about two miles distant. They were supported by six pieces of artillery.[5]

The next morning the Federals advanced against this line and drove it back after considerable fighting. Evans arrived about ten o'clock and assumed command, placing Radcliffe in command on the left. As soon as he arrived Evans decided to attempt to hold back the Federals. Although it seemed a hopeless task, he realized that if Goldsboro was to be saved he would have to hold Foster until reinforcements arrived. The Federals pushed forward slowly during the day and drove the Confederates to within two miles of the Kinston bridge. At this point, the two armies bivouacked for the night, the Confederates sleeping on their weapons.[6]

Early on the morning of the fifteenth, Radcliffe notified Evans that he had been attacked. In the meantime, the Holcombe Legion and Colonel Peter Mallet's North Carolina Battalion had reinforced Evans, increasing his command to 2,014 men. Evans ordered Radcliffe to hold his position, while Evans attacked Foster's left. The Confederates advanced but met stiff opposition from the Federals. After engaging the Federals for nearly three hours, the Confederates fell back to the Kinston bridge. The Confederates made a determined stand at the bridge but were forced to retire, setting fire to the bridge as they crossed. Over four hundred men, however, were unable to withdraw and were captured.[7]

During the engagement, Evans was in the thick of the fight, encouraging his men by leading. While the fighting was going on at the bridge, he was an excellent target for the Federal Sharpshooters, and bullets barely missed him as he walked about giving orders to his troops. And, in fact, he had a very narrow escape while sitting on a rail of the bridge. A shell struck the rail on which he was sitting but the missile sped on and buried itself in the ground, sparing Evans.[8]

Extinguishing the flames at the bridge, the Northern troops pushed on to Kinston under the cover of the fire of their powerful artillery. Evans retreated for about two miles along the Goldsboro road and then formed a line of battle. During the retreat, Evans was reinforced by Colonel S. H. Rogers's 47th Regiment North Carolina State Troops.[9]

At three o'clock in the afternoon, General Foster, who attended West Point with Evans and was a close friend before the war, sent Colonel Edward E. Potter to ask Evans if he was ready to surrender.

> *Officer.* "I understand, sir, (bowing) that some of your troops have indicated a wish to surrender, and I have been detached to receive the surrender by Gen. Foster. I presume, sir, that you are Gen. Evans?"
>
> *Gen. E.* "I am – who are you sir?"
>
> *Officer.* (With a supercilious sir) "I am Col. Potter, sir, of the 1st North Carolina Volunteers, and attached to the staff of Gen. Foster."
>
> *Gen. E.* "I am not aware, sir, that any of my troops desire to surrender, nor do I believe there is a South Carolinian under my command who has any intention of doing so. Give my compliments to Gen. Foster, and tell him that he knows Gen. Evans too well to suppose that he will ever surrender."
>
> *Col. P.* "Then you intend to renew the battle."
>
> *Gen. E.* "Yes, sir, — *to fight now and here.*"
>
> *Col. P.* "Do you mean to begin at once, sir, or do you wish time to remove your wounded?"
>
> *Gen. E.* "Well, sir, you may say to Gen. Foster that if he will give me an hour and a half to remove the women and children from the town, I shall then be ready for him!"

Several newspapers, however, reported that Evans's reply to Foster was a simple and succinct, "Go to Hell."[10]

Foster delayed the attack about an hour in order to get his artillery across the bridge. In the meantime, Evans fell back to Falling Creek where he met reinforcements consisting of two North Carolina regiments and six hundred dismounted cavalrymen under the command of Brigadier-General Beverly H. Robertson. Because it was now sundown, and the terrain at Falling Creek afforded a strong defensive position, Evans decided to bivouac there for the night.[11]

Early the following morning Evans hurriedly issued a report of his present situation to General Cooper.

> Kinston, N. C.,
>
> December 14, 1862
>
> General Foster attacked Kinston yesterday with 15,000 men and nine gunboats. I fought him ten hours. Have driven back his gunboats. His army is still in my front. I have only four regiments, and will await his attack this morning. I think I can hold my position.
>
> N. G. Evans,
>
> Brigadier-General[12]

On the morning of the fifteenth, Foster recrossed the Neuse and proceeded in the direction of Goldsboro. Having learned of this movement, Evans dispatched Robertson with the 11th Regiment North Carolina State Troops and six hundred dismounted cavalrymen to prevent the Federals from crossing at White Hall. At the same time, Evans sent Colonel Rogers's regiment to Kinston, holding his own brigade in readiness to move to the support of either Robertson or Rogers. Learning that Foster had recrossed the Neuse and burned the bridge, Evans retired to Mosely Hall to support Robertson. Evans was met at this point by Major-General Samuel G. French, the commander of the department, who assumed command and sent reinforcements to Robertson.[13]

Robertson arrived at White Hall on the fifteenth and burned the bridge across the Neuse as soon as he heard that the Federals were approaching. The next day, he engaged the Northern troops and prevented their crossing. Failing to cross at White Hall, Foster continued his advance toward Goldsboro and encamped that night about eight miles away from the town.[14]

After the Federals were repulsed at White Hall, French ordered Evans to report to General Gustavus W. Smith at Goldsboro. On the morning of the seventeenth, Smith sent Evans to take command of a force composed of Brigadier-General Thomas L. Clingman's brigade and Evans's brigade with which he was to make an armed reconnaissance of the Federals approaching the railroad bridge. At this time, a dispatch arrived from Clingman's command stationed at the county and railroad bridges that the Federals were within three miles of the bridge.[15]

The county bridge was about half a mile up the Neuse from the railroad bridge, and the road crossing it ran nearly parallel to the railroad. There was a swamp between the two bridges but the infantry were able to advance without difficulty along the banks of the Neuse.[16]

Clingman's brigade consisted of three regiments and two guns of J. B. Starr's battery. Clingman had stationed one regiment at each bridge and one between, so that it could support the most vulnerable point. As soon as the Federals commenced firing on the regiment at the railroad bridge, Clingman sent the regiment stationed between the bridges to support it. The Confederates held their position for some time, but the heavy artillery fire of the powerful Federal batteries forced them to retire to the county bridge. Evans impressed upon Clingman the necessity of holding the county bridge, assuring him that the railroad bridge was secure. Not long afterward, however, the Federals set fire to the railroad bridge. After the bridge was in flames, the Federal batteries ceased firing and Foster gave orders for the command to retire. In the meantime, Evans had ordered an advance. The Confederates occupied the railroad line and then launched an attack upon the Federals, who retreated to a higher field in front of the them where their batteries began to play upon the charging Rebels. The Confederates made a gallant assault upon the Federals in this new position, but were repulsed. As it was now almost dark, they made no further attempt to drive the Federals from this position. Having succeeded in cutting the railroad, Foster retired during the night and began his retreat to Kinston.[17]

The Federal losses for the campaign were 92 killed, 487 wounded, and 12 missing or captured. There is no available list of the Confederate losses, but they were greater than the Federal's because of the large number of prisoners taken at the Kinston bridge.[18]

On the twentieth Evans submitted his official report on the Goldsboro campaign.

Headquarters Evans' Brigade,
Near Goldsborough [sic], N. C., December 20, 1862

MAJOR: I have the honor to submit the following report of the action of the troops under my command in the recent engagements near Kinston, White Hall, and at the railroad bridge near this place:

On Saturday, the 13th instant, the enemy approached Kinston in considerable force and attacked the line of our forces under the immediate command of Col. James D. Radcliffe, North Carolina Troops, who had taken position on the west side of Southwest Creek. At 10 o'clock I arrived on the ground and assumed command, and ordered Colonel Radcliffe to take command of the left wing at the crossing of the upper Trent road. The enemy then was attacked at Hines' Mill while he attempted to cross the creek. After a sharp engagement of an hour I fell back toward the Neuse River, keeping line of battle and arresting his approach about 2 miles from Kinston Bridge. He then attacked in considerable force, but retired after an engagement of ten hours. I rested on my arms that night in this position, the enemy ceasing fire after nightfall.

On the morning of the 14th (Sunday), being informed by Colonel Radcliffe that the enemy was approaching his position, I directed him to open fire while I would attack his left. I ordered an immediate advance, and soon became engaged with my whole line with the enemy in heavy force – supposed to be about 20,000. The action lasted about three hours, when, ascertaining his greatly superior force, I retired with my command across the Neuse Bridge, when the enemy pursued with heavy fire, stormed the bridge, and drove me back to the town of Kinston, capturing about 400, including no sick prisoners. Reforming my line, with the additional re-enforcements of Col. [S. H.] Rogers' Forty seventh Regiment North Carolina Troops, in a commanding position in rear of the town, I again awaited the attack. About 3 P.M. Major-General Foster sent his staff officer (Colonel Potter) to summon me to surrender, which I promptly declined. In an hour he commenced shelling the town, but hesitated to renew his direct attack. Taking advantage of my position, I retired in column to Falling Creek, where the major-general commanding had forwarded me additional re-enforcements. At this point (a very strong position) I encamped for the night. Hearing early next morning that the enemy had recrossed the river and was advancing on White Hall in my rear, I immediately dispatched one regiment (the Eleventh North Carolina Troops, Col. [C.] Leventhorpe) and 600 dismounted cavalry, the whole under the command of Brig. Gen. B. H. Robertson, to proceed in haste and dispute his crossing at White Hall, while I would attack his rear toward Kinston. The report of Brigadier-General Robertson is herewith inclosed, marked A. I here sent Colonel Rogers to march on Kinston, and held my other forces in readiness to move in either direction. Finding the enemy had retired across the river and burned the bridge, I ordered my whole command to Mosely Hall, a position where I could support General Robertson. At this point I met Major-General French, commanding department, who immediately assumed command and timely re-enforced Brigadier-General Robertson. My force engaged at Kinston consisted of the Seventeenth, Twenty-second, Twenty-third and Holcombe Legion South Carolina Volunteers; Colonel Radcliffe's 61st Regiment North Carolina Troops; Major Mallett's battalion; Capt. [R.] Boyce's light battery South Carolina Volunteers; Captains Bunting's and Starr's batteries North Carolina troops. Lieutenant-Colonel Pool, commanding North Carolina heavy artillery, commanded the intrenchments at the obstructions below Kinston and attacked the gunboats and held them in check while I regained my position in rear of the town. My whole force amounted to 2,014.

From Mosely Hall (after the repulse of the enemy at White Hall) I was directed by the major-general commanding the department to report to Goldsborough. On my arrival with my command was ordered by Maj. Gen. G. W. Smith to assume command of Brig. Gen. T. L. Clingman's brigade and make an armed reconnaissance of the enemy approaching the railroad bridge. I immediately ordered General Clingman to advance his brigade over the river by the country bridge and engage him; that I would support his left. On arriving beyond the bridge about a mile General Clingman became engaged with the enemy in heavy force. I directed Evans' brigade to advance to his support. On reaching the railroad I found the enemy drawn up in line of battle marching up to the railroad. I then directed my brigade to cross the railroad and engage the enemy, which was done in a spirited manner. I also herewith inclose General Clingman's report, together with a list of killed and wounded.

In conclusion I would call the attention of the major-general commanding to the gallant conduct and admirable judgement of Colonel Radcliffe, who had disposed his troops to dispute every advance of the enemy, and regret to add that, holding his position to the last of the fight, he was taken prisoner, but readily paroled. The following officers were observed by myself as conspicuous in the battles of Saturday and Sunday: Col. P. Mallett, North Carolina Troops; Capt. [M. G.] Zeigler, Holcombe Legion; Adjt. W. P. Du Bose, wounded while leading his regiment; Capt. [S. A.] Durham, [Company H], Twenty-third South Carolina Volunteers, wounded severely leading his regiment in action at the railroad.

To the promptness of General Clingman in obeying my orders I am particularly indebted for the repulse at the railroad near Goldsborough.

To my personal staff (Capt. A. L. Evans and 1st Lieut. Samuel J. Corrie, aide-de-camp) I am much indebted, both for the intrepidity and alacrity with which they obeyed my orders, both often leading troops in action. I recommend both to the especial attention of the major-general commanding. Col. John A. Baker, 44th [41st] North Carolina Troops, deserves especial notice; though suffering with a slight wound, was very energetic as my assistant through the engagements of the two days.

Colonels Radcliffe and Mallett being paroled prisoners, the reports of their respective commands will be forwarded as soon as exchanged.

Herewith please find list [not found] of killed and wounded

in my brigade. The lists from the other commands have not been furnished me.

Very respectfully submitted.

N. G. Evans,
Brigadier-General, Commanding

Maj. S. W. Melton,
Assistant Adjutant-General, Goldsborough, N. C.[19]

The press in North and South Carolina gave considerable space to the Federal invasion. At the time, many people thought that the real object of the invasion was to take Goldsboro and then to proceed farther toward the interior of the state. The papers highly praised Evans and those who fought with him for stopping the Federal advance. There were some friendly disagreements in the press about different movements and the officers who deserved credit for them. There was also a disagreement as to whether Evans or Clingman was to blame for allowing the Federals to set fire to the railroad bridge near Goldsboro. One correspondent, "Personne," stated that the reason Evans could not save the bridge was that the train that was carrying his brigade arrived too late for the brigade to defend the bridge.[20]

"Personne" was also profuse in his praise of Evans after the battle. In speaking of the engagement at Kinston, he related:

> This is the only instance during the war where a Confederate General has been bold enough to oppose the Abolitionists when the odds were ten to one. But it was done by Evans here, and if necessary will be done again and again. His motto is 'to fight the enemy wherever he can find them' and if he is compelled to retreat in the language of his order 'fall back fighting.' It was the very temerity of Evans' attack here, with a mere handful of troops, which disconcerted Foster, and made him so wary during his march to Goldsboro, and to this day, as I am informed by citizens of Kinston, believe that the Confederate force was not less than ten thousand strong. The entire credit of this portion of the campaign belongs to General Evans.[21]

There were some who criticized the generalship that Evans displayed at Kinston. They asserted that the South Carolinian made a grave mistake by offering battle on the opposite bank of the Neuse against so large a force. "Personne," however, countered that if Evans had not given battle to Foster across the Neuse and delayed him for twenty-four hours, Foster would have proceeded as he did up the other bank of the Neuse and would have taken Goldsboro before reinforcements could arrive.[22]

Evans remained at Kinston until about the middle of February 1863, but during this time the Federals did not attempt another invasion. On several occasions they annoyed his pickets, and at times Evans, thinking that Foster would move against him, asked for reinforcements. But, with the exception of the picket skirmishes there was little fighting.[23]

Evans, however, had other things with which to contend that affected him personally and caused him much more anxiety than the Federals. On December 25, he stated in a letter to his wife that "the rascal Col. McMaster has attempted to disaffect the Brigade against me, thinking that I am too rash. I have him now under arrest and will keep him so." Fitzhugh W. McMaster and Colonel S. D. Goodlet continued to circulate reports that were derogatory to Evans's character, claiming that Evans had been drunk during the battle on numerous occasions. These reports hurt Evans deeply. And, after due consideration of the matter, he asked for a Court of Inquiry, demanding that the persons spreading the malicious reports bring formal charges against him. Charges were finally brought by Goodlet, but the court-martial did not convene until February.[24] In the meantime, the rumors spread through South Carolina that Evans had been removed from his command and that charges had been brought against him on the grounds of incompetence, cowardice, and intoxication. Hearing that South Carolina was filled with such rumors, "Personne" came to Evans's defense. On January 6, in a lengthy rebuttal, he acknowledged that charges had been made against Evans by one of his colonels, but, in fact, Evans had not been deprived of his command.

> . . . In standing between General Evans and the public, and setting forth facts that ought to counteract the influence of these

rumors – facts which General Evans or no other officer in his position could properly communicate — my only object is to do justice in the promises to one who has never yet reflected aught but honor upon his native State, and then to let the future take care of itself. I predict that the future will leave his fame as untarnished as his sword.

The reputation of a soldier is as dear to him as is virtue to a woman. And like virtue it requires but a breath of suspicion to mar its purity. Has General Evans deserved all this from the public? Has he been incompetent? Commence with his career among the Indians of New Mexico. Why did South Carolina vote him a costly sword of the value of ten thousand dollars? Follow him from Fort Sumter to Manassas, where his little command of a few hundred men met and sustained the first shock of battle, until the remainder of our forces could be got into position. Was it because of his 'incompetency' there, that the President conferred upon him one of the earliest appointments as Brigadier-General? Was it because of 'incompetency' that he was next transferred to the important command of Leesburg – the chief gate-way to the rear of our army – where, by able generalship he held in check ten thousand of the enemy at one point while he was inflicting a terrible punishment on five thousand elsewhere – a blow that made the North howl with rage, and the South exult in gladness? Was it owing to 'incompetency' that, soon after this event, he was invested with the command of a division, which he retained until ordered to this place; and was held by General Lee, subject to special duty, outside of the regular line of division movements, and, finally, did his 'Incompetency' display itself here, where with two thousand and fourteen men he met twenty thousand of the Abolitionists, held them in check for a day and a half, and but for superior orders would have been in their rear? History has written the answer; the proof is upon the record; there let it stand.

The evidence of the 'cowardice' of Gen. Evans are as abundant as the examples of his 'incompetency.' Among the most prominent of these is, when a Captain in the United States Army, he met four Indians in a hand to hand encounter and killed them all. Further on we find him again at Manassas in the thickest of the fight. At Boonesboro Gap, Captain T. D. Eason, standing as one of his aids, is wounded by a musket ball, while standing in a few feet of him. At Sharpsburg, young Fauquier Trezevant is mortally wounded almost by his side. On the Rappahannock, his Orderly has his horse killed while following the General, and the latter exposes himself so rashly that General Stevens, then of the Holcombe Legion, remonstrates with him because of his imprudence. At the second Manassas he occupies a position within seven hundred yards of the enemy's batteries, which are pouring forth a steady volume of grape and canister: and at Kinston he dismounts from his horse, and for an hour or more walks calmly on the river bank, the mark of the Yankee rifles and artillery.

The most serious charge and the one most likely to affect the personal character of the General, because oftenest repeated, is that of drunkenness. Yet as far as my experience extends – and it has been by no means a limited one – I believe this allegation even less reliable than its two predecessors. It has been my fortune during the past year to meet General Evans and the officers of his staff frequently. I have seen him in the dawn of morning, in the flush of noon, and at the hour of retirement, before battle, during battle and after battle, but never on any occasion when it could be said that he was drunk – drunk entirely or drunk approximately.

That he has his faults, and among others an impetuosity of character and nervousness of disposition that cannot brook disappointment – disobedience of orders, and above all a retreat of his men, which finds vent in flashing eye, strong language, and passionate gestures, I am free to admit, but this is not drunkenness not withstanding those who know Evans the least may so pronounce.

I have heard it said that his orderly carries with him, whenever he follows his chief, a small two-quart cask of liquor from which the General draws his rations. This is true; but there is something more touchingly true of that little cask, still. A badly wounded man, be it friend or foe, has never passed it by without a draft of its contents. Three times at the battle of Manassas, and several times at Sharpsburg, was it emptied and refilled, and them emptied again among the feeble ones who lay bleeding on the ground, the General himself dismounting, and on bending knee applying gratefully relief to the parched lips. "A drop for me, General, if you have got it," moaned poor Col. Means, and in a moment more he was lifted into life, and so strengthened that he could be carried from the field. Capt. Seabrook, too, lay dying there, with the brains gushing out from his forehead. And again the flask was made to perform its charitable work in bathing the pale face and moistening the lips of the sufferer.

Scores of such instances might be narrated, and if the half were told, instead of the sweeping charges of drunkenness – some of them almost severe enough to be maledictions – you would hear thousands bless the man who, amid the roar of battle, could so humanely blend the high responsibilities of a commanding officer with the tender remembrance of the dying soldiers around him.

It is too late in the day to deprive an officer of his hard earned reputation who for fifteen years has carried his life in his hand, to be yielded up for the public good whenever the sacrifice might be demanded, and who has twice received the testimonials from the Legislature of his own State, and the thanks of Mississippi and the Confederate Congress.

I am aware that I have written warmly, but not more so than the circumstances demanded; and not more so than shall always be the case when I can wield a pen to right a wrong.[25]

"Personne" was not the only one who came to Evans's aid. Captain John Hillary Gary stated publicly in Charleston that if any man attempted to spread false rumors concerning General Evans's habits he would hold him accountable.[26]

At the convening of the court-martial on February 2, 1863, Goodlet brought the following charges against Evans:

Charge Drunkenness

1st Specification – . . . Evans on the 14th day of September, 1862 at Boonsboro Maryland . . . was so much intoxicated that he was unfit for the discharge of his duties.

2nd Specification – . . . Evans . . . about the 6th Nov. 1862 when his Brigade was being transported by the cars from Culpeper Virginia, appeared in the state of intoxication before a number of his men.

3rd Specification – . . . Evans at Halifax in the State of North

Carolina on or about the 11th day of November 1862 was intoxicated.

4th Specification – . . . Evans at Kinston North Carolina on the 14th. day of December 1862, while his Brigade was retreating from the enemy, was intoxicated.[27]

Colonel F. W. McMaster, the principal witness against Evans, bore the brunt of Evans's attack. Evans assailed his character in the following detailed manner:

Col. F. W. McMaster the real author of the charges before the Court, the principal witness for the prosecution, testifies that he has been watching my conduct with the strictest scrutiny for months. 'That he was of the impression that I was intoxicated because my face was red, and that I ordered his regiment to slacken its march while I was going into action, and to bring his regiment into line of battle in good order.' This at Boonsboro.' At Kinston he says 'I had a peculiar look, ' tho' I gave what he calls the proper orders.' The character of this witness should not be overlooked. He bears the reputation in the brigade of that of an Elder of the Church who is remarkable for being engaged in his devotional exercises when his regiment is engaged with the enemy. The battle of Kinston is the only engagement where this example of piety was ever under my immediate command, and in this engagement [he] refused to fight the enemy. At the battle of Boonsboro, thinking that he would not be observed, and taking advantage of the woods and rocks (boulders) he ignobly fled from his regiment and attempted to conceal his person from the observation of his Commanding General by hiding behind a large rock, a quarter of a mile from and in rear of his regiment, who were warmly engaged with the foe lying prostrate on the ground in his place of concealment. It was with difficulty that his Commanding General could induce him to do his duty. For which offense he is now under charges connected with those of conduct unbecoming an officer and a gentleman. Lying, making false reports, concealing desertion etc.[28]

The Court of Inquiry asked several officers who were associated with Evans in past campaigns to write letters concerning his character. Major T. D. Eason's response to the Court of Inquiry praised the general in no uncertain terms:

> Your esteemed favor of the 6th was not received by me until last night, & hasten to reply to your inquiries respecting my knowledge of Genl. Evans habits. I was attached to his Staff from the 5th Jan. 1862 until October of the same year, and believe more intimately connected with him, than any member of his staff, & can unhesitatingly say, that I never saw him in a condition to unfit him for business. At Boonsboro I was on the field with him all the time, he being perfectly cool & extended his orders as usual, until his men began to fall back, & he then became excited, & rode among them endeavoring to rally them, with the rest of us, & remember distinctly of Private Dean 22nd Regt. calling on the men to rally around the General on that occasion. I never saw General Evans in a condition that he could not walk or ride perfectly well, & attend to all his business. He may perhaps drink more than does him good at times but he certainly is not a drunkard, & hope the Court may find him innocent of the charge. He is naturally an excitable man, & believe many times, excitement has been mistaken for intoxication. It would grieve me much to know that the charge was sustained, as I believe I know him as well as any other man, & had better opportunities of judging his character than most men, & from my personal acquaintance with him would pronounce him a kind hearted, courageous & good soldier & never so happy as when the enemy was in his front. I had heard that the Court had exonerated him from the charges, which gave me so much pleasure & hope it may prove so.[29]

The Court of Inquiry rendered its decision in February 1863. In part, the official report read:

> The statement of the accused being thus in position of the Court, the Court was then cleared for deliberation, and having maturely considered the evidence added, find the accused, Brigadier-General N. G. Evans, P.A.C.S. –
> Of the first specification – not guilty
> Of the second specification – not guilty
> Of the third specification – not guilty

Of the fourth specification – not guilty

Of the charge – not guilty

The accused, Brigadier general N. G. Evans, P.A.C.S. is therefore, fully acquitted of the charge and specifications preferred against him.

R. E. Colston

Brig. Gen. Pres't. Court of Inquiry

Thos. C. Fuller, 1st. Lieutenant Company B., N.C. T. Judge Advocate

The Court deem it their duty to express their opinion that the author of these charges could not have been influenced, in preferring them, by the good of the service, but must have been instigated by a malicious and wrongful spirit, and such conduct is considered highly reprehensible and prejudicial to good order and military discipline.

R. E. Colston

Brig. Gen. Pres't Court of Inquiry[30]

A number of Southern newspapers printed articles congratulating Evans on his vindication by the Court of Inquiry. One Southern journal pointedly made this comment: "Without undertaking in the absence of the testimony adduced on the occasion to express any opinion we cannot forbear expressing the hope that Col. Goodlet, and the other malcontents who were instrumental in instigating those proceedings will remember the closing remarks of the court in their judgment upon the case."[31]

Evans received letters of congratulations from numerous friends through the South. Among these was a letter from Paul Hamilton Hayne, the noted South Carolina poet, who wrote Evans on March 8, 1863:

> I heard some time ago, with pain, & indignation that certain charges had been preferred against you, & that a Court Martial was about to examine, & decide upon the case.
>
> In common with *all* your friends, I never doubted for a moment, what the issue of a fair trial would be, & this confidence, (thank Heaven!) has been more than justified. I really think *General*, that your enemies have done you good service. The State respected, & loved you before, but this unworthy per-

secution, this unworthy attempt to strip your brow of its laurels, must only result in adding tenfold to your reputation.

When the news of your triumphant acquittal, reached me, I was seized by an irresistible impulse to commemorate the result in verse. Consequently, I set to work, & composed the *Poem*, which I now have the honor of presenting to you. If deficient in *Art*, it is believe me, *most sincere.*

All my family are true admirers of yours. My little *wife* especially, take great interest in your career, begs me to say that she congratulates you upon your brilliant vindication. She is a sister of your old surgeon, and warm friend, Dr. Fraser Michel. And now, trusting that your future pathway may be unclouded, I am *General*

Faithfully yours,
Paul H. Hayne

P. S. Pray, give my regards to *Mrs.* Evans, — I hope your noble '*little boy,*' (I saw him last spring at 'Adams Run') is a hearty, & strong as he promised to be. By he way, the *enclosed poem* has been sent to a prominent Richmond journal, & when published, I shall try & procure for you a *printed* copy.[32]

EVANS

The trial past, the ordeal done,
Thou standest in the noonday sun
Of clear renown, — with spotless name
And radiant in thy patriot fame;
No blast of Scorn, no string of Hate
Henceforth shall cloud or blight thy fate;
A people's Love, a people's Pride,
Shall guard thee o'ver the battle-tide,
And ne'er shall Slander's air of death
Pollute thee with its poisoned breath!

Frank soldier! I behold thee now,
With gallant mien and lifted brow,
The glow of conscious virtue shed
About they form and o'er thy head;
Detraction shuddering, shrinks away,
Pierced by the keen Ithuriel ray

Of Truth, — while freed from taint or stain
Stern in they manhood's strength again,
The lustre of they knightly brand
Grows brighter in that firm right hand.

Hero of Leesburg! – thou whose might,
And valor in the desperate fight,
Backed by they faithful Southrons, hurled
Our foemen to the under-world, —
Lighting with victory' splendid blaze,
The darkness of those mournful days, —[33]
Oh! Deem not, while a deadlier foe
Aimed at thy breast the ruthless blow,
They Country coldly watched apart
The torturing of thy noble heart.

No! in a thousand spirits burned
A quenchless sympathy, that yearned
To soothe three in the manly grief,
And cheer thee with calm Belief
Which nurtured by thy glorious deeds,
Had spring to flower from golden seeds, —
Assured whate'er the stealthy word,
Or open menaces they heard,
Thy eagle soul would grandly rise,
Full-plumed thro' Honor's kindling skies!

Hero of Kinston! – not in vain
Hath wrought they sword, hath toiled they brain –
Our Mother-Dand, sublimely true,
Where all her trust and praise are due,
Shall greet thee with her tenderest grace,
Shall fold thee in her close embrace –
Her loving arms around thee thrown,
Her great heart throbbing next thine own,
Who – who – this matchless tribute won –
Dare strike the Mother thro' her son?[34]

Since the early part of the year Evans had been encouraging several friends who were members of the Confederate Congress to make appeals in his behalf so that he might be promoted to the rank of major-general. After his acquittal by the Court of Inquiry, he sent the verdict of the court to these friends in Richmond. He received an encouraging letter from Senator Albert Gallatin Brown of Mississippi in early March:

> I recd. your note covering the 'Extract' with the liveliest satisfaction. I had a moral conviction from the first that no court would ever convict you of any conduct unbecoming an officer a soldier or a gentleman. But it was gratifying to know that you had been acquitted and your accuser rebuked in such pointed terms by the Court- Capt. Singleton has gone to North Carolina on a brief visit to his family who are residing there temporarily. When he comes we will unite in asking the President to give you that promotion which we both think you so richly merit. Meantime I will get Mr. Orr and some of the other South Carolinians to move on the matter.
>
> If there is anything in either of my letters which you think will be of service to you if made public you have my consent to publish it.[35]

Brown wrote Evans again on March 8, enclosing his and O. R. Singleton's letter to President Davis in Evans's behalf:

> The foregoing is a copy of the letter which Capt. Singleton & myself have addressed to the President. Cap. S. desires me to say that he signed it with sincere pleasure. I handed it to Mr. Orr who has prepared an application to the President for your promotion. He will hand all the papers to the President and some of us will see him in person on the subject from time to time and so keep it before him.[36]

Brown and Singleton's letter to President Davis was extremely complimentary of Evans:

> We understand that the friends of Brig. Gen. N. G. Evans are about to invite your attention to what they regard as his just claims to promotion. We were for a few months under the command of

Genl. Evans and feel it to be both a privilege and a duty to speak of him as we saw him. Of his skill as a commander we perhaps are not competent judges. But so far as we are capable of judging we do not hesitate to say that in the battle of Leesburg where we were with him, he displayed the highest evidences of Generalship. One great quality for a commander we know Gentl. Evans possesses in a very high degree, that of attaching his soldiers to him. His discipline is mild and parental but firm and decided. While we were with him we saw every day almost every hour the strongest proofs of his firm hold on the affections of his men. Of his courage we have no occasion to speak, that has been put beyond question on too many bloody fields to require endorsement now.

We have heard of but one ground of serous objection to the Promotion of Genl. Evans and that is the charge of *drunkenness*. Of course, we can only reply to this charge so far as knew him and had full and fair opportunities of judging. From the time we passed under his command in July 1861 until we left the army in November & did afterwards, we know and therefore affirm that the charge is not sustained by the facts. It has been asserted that Genl. Evans was drunk at the battle of Leesburg. This we flatly contradict on our own personal knowledge and observation. We do not deny that the General sometimes drinks, probably he may sometimes take more than is prudent. But that he becomes intoxicated or in any degree incapacitated for business we do not believe.

We have only to add that the promotion of our old commander would gratify us exceedingly.[37]

About the same time, Evans received a letter from W. Porcher Miles, a member of Congress from South Carolina, which was not so encouraging as the ones he had received from Brown. In speaking of the possibility of Evans's promotion, Miles said: "Genl. McQueen will speak to the Secretary about your promotion, he tells me. I shall be happy to co-operate with him. I have longed ceased to attempt to get the President to promote or appoint anyone. He has so often ignored the warmly expressed wish and earnest recommendation of the entire delegation that my self-respect forbids my approaching him."[38]

On March 15, John McQueen wrote Evans:

I duly recd. your favor of the 30th. Jany. & fear you will think I have been very remiss in delaying so long to answer, but aside from the rule I have generally practiced, to only write when necessity demands or I can accomplish something of value to my friends; when I recd. your letter your case was pending upon charges made against you, painful I have no doubt to you, as I assure you they were to your friends, and I did not think it worth while to make any move for your promotion until your case was disposed of.

Immediately after recd. information of your triumphant acquittal, (upon which allow me sincerely to congratulate you) Col. Orr wrote an application to the President for your promotion. Signed it himself when I took it, & with my own signature obtained the signatures of Messrs. Miles, Simpson, & Boyce & would have presented it in person but the President was taken sick & confined to his room for some week or upwards. As soon as he recovered so as to be able to attend to business I sought a personal interview with him, & on the third trial (being everyday engaged with his Cabinet) I obtained a full opportunity & presented your claims, with the writing above, accompanied by a strong letter from Gov. Brown, Col. Singleton being absent with a sick family, I put your claims upon your record in the war and the date of your commission as Brigdr. He made no pledge to me, & upon the fact that others junior to you have been promoted he showed me a long list of many senior to you in the army generally & Ripley, Drayton & some others of So. Ca., but said that there are no vacancies for Majr. Genls. at present & that he rather thought he had more at present in the army than there was necessity for. I left the papers with him after a full conversation with him leaving him to act of course as he will do, according to his own notion of right.

I thus dear Genl. have given you a full account of my efforts for you; & feel that I have done all that I can in the premises; What it may avail you I cannot say. You may excuse me when I say to you that I would not be surprised, if the charges & talk on the subject of your drinking, may be some what an impediment in your way; though I do not say so, from a word or indication from the President in our interview, but simply from my own notion of human nature, however unjust the charges might be. I hope that your career may continue as bright through the war as it has been heretofore and you may survive the perils & conflicts yet to encounter.[39]

Yet Evans did not give up hope. In April, while in Richmond on official business, he asked Senator James L. Orr to approach Davis on the subject. On April 9, Orr wrote: "I have seen the President once since you left here. I called his attention to your promotion. He said there were no vacancies. He made no other objection but made no promise. I will see him again upon the subject before we adjourn which will perhaps be in two weeks."[40]

Although cleared by the court, Evans felt rebuffed by the Confederate high command. For the rest of the war, he continued to push for that elusive promotion. He no doubt believed that his troubles concerning his well-deserved promotion stemmed from "the rascal Col. McMaster." The two remained as enemies for the duration of their lives and then the feud continued through Evans's son, who became a political enemy of McMaster and who eventually went on to be governor of South Carolina.

In the early part of February, Evans was ordered to leave Kinston and report to another post in North Carolina. Upon hearing of this, about fifty male residents of Kinston signed the following petition:

> We the undersigned, citizens of Kinston, having learned that orders have been received relieving Brigadier General N. G. Evans from command of this Post, take the opportunity of expressing the regret felt by the entire community in parting with one in whom we have such entire confidence and who by his skill, bravery and energetic action in the late affair with the enemy at this place on the 13th and 14th of December last, succeeded in checking the advance of an overwhelming force to invade this State.
>
> We cheerfully bear testimony to his gallantry as an officer, and courtesy as a gentleman, and his conduct of operations in this quarter, have restored confidence and relieve industry from fear of invasion.[41]

On February 10, Evans replied to the petition:

Gentlemen: Your complimentary letter was received be me yesterday. I feel a soldier's pride in having this assurance of your confidence and it gives me pleasure to say that the duties of my command were greatly lightened by the hearty-cooperation of the citizens of your vicinity and my stay among you, made agreeable by the kindness of those who you represent – your wives, sisters, daughters and mothers, to myself and my command.

If the enemy shall again threaten you, I will gladly obey the order to hasten to your protection.[42]

After leaving Kinston, Evans's brigade was placed in the District of Cape Fear, which was commanded by Brigadier-General W. H. C. Whiting. This district formed a part of the Department of North Carolina and Virginia and was under the command of General Longstreet. Evans served in this district at different posts until around April 11, 1863, when his brigade was ordered to Charleston, which was facing the prospects of a serious Federal attack. Whiting, however, was reluctant to part with Evans's brigade unless he could get a brigade in its place. For several weeks the situation remained in doubt, but in the latter part of April, Evans was definitely assigned to Charleston with John R. Cooke's brigade replacing his brigade at Wilmington. Evans was excited at the prospects of going home.[43]

Bust of Nathan Evans outside Vicksburg High School, Vicksburg, Mississippi. The existence of this bust and the monument on the next page is testimonial to the "Tramp Brigade's" considerable movement throughout the Civil War.

Sculptor: Louis Millione; erected in 1914.

(Photo courtesy of Don Hill)

Monument to South Carolina troops under the command of
Evans at Vicksburg. Located outside Vicksburg High School, Vicksburg,
Mississippi, it was dedicated in 1935.

(Photo courtesy of Don Hill)

Evans's final resting place in Tabernacle Cemetery located between Cokesburg and Greenwood, SC. General Martin Witherspoon Gary Evans's brother-in-law, is buried in this cemetery as well.

(Photos by Jason Silverman)

Captain Nathan
Evans during the
Mexican War era.
(Photo courtesy of
The South
Caroliniana Library)

General Nathan Evans
during the Civil War.
(Photo courtesy of the
Evans Family)

John H. Gary Evans, son of
Nathan Evans and governor
of South Carolina in 1894.
(Photo courtesy of The South
Caroliniana Library)

Anne Victoria ("Vic") Gary
Evans, wife of Nathan
Evans and sister of General
Martin Gary.
(Photo courtesy of the
Evans Family)

General Martin Witherspoon
Gary, Evans's brother-in-law.
(Photos courtesy of The South
Caroliniana Library)

Colonel Fitzhugh William McMaster (1826-1899), Evans's arch nemesis.
(Photo courtesy of The South Caroliniana Library)

David Jackson Logan, member of The "Tramp Brigade" and lieutenant in the 17th South Carolina Volunteers, who wrote extensively about Nathan Evans. (Photo courtesy of the Logan Family)

General Pierre Gustave Toutant Beauregard (Photo courtesy of the National Archives)

— Chapter IX —

VICKSBURG

After an absence of nine months, Evans was again stationed at Charleston. During his time away, the Federals had been threatening both Savannah and Charleston but had met with little success. The Federals had succeeded, however, in capturing Fort Pulaski near Savannah, and had assumed control of the waters surrounding the islands near Charleston. In April 1863, the Federal fleet attempted to subdue Fort Sumter, but was driven off by the Confederate coastal batteries and withdrew to Port Royal for repairs. After this repulse, the Union Navy confined its activities to pillaging and raiding the planters along the coastal rivers.

The Federals had been more successful in the West. General Ulysses S. Grant with a powerful army was now threatening Vicksburg, Mississippi. It appeared that the Confederates would have to send reinforcements to aid John C. Pemberton at Vicksburg and that Beauregard, in command at Charleston, would be called upon for some of the needed reinforcements. On May 1, Evans wrote home that

> There is a rumor that the fancy troops who have been vege-
> tating here for the last two years will be sent to the West or to
> Virginia where I think they ought to go in order to know what
> the war is. Gist will be ordered off. He pretends he is anxious to

go but I do not believe him . . . The news is not favorable this morning as the enemy seems to be moving both in Virginia and in the West. I think however we are prepared for him in both places. Tho' I think we should reinforce Genl. Johnston in Tennessee . . . .[1]

The rumors proved to be true. The following day, James A. Seddon, Confederate secretary of war, telegraphed Beauregard that the Federals had given up operations on the coast and were concentrating large forces in the West. He ordered Beauregard to send as many as ten thousand men immediately to Pemberton's aid in Vicksburg. Beauregard replied that he could send five thousand troops and two light batteries, but if he sent more he would not be able to protect the Savannah-Charleston Railroad. This satisfied Seddon, who instructed Beauregard to dispatch the soldiers at once. Accordingly, Beauregard ordered W. H. T. Walker's and Gist's brigades to proceed to Mississippi.

The situation in Mississippi quickly became critical. On May 9, Seddon telegraphed Beauregard to send five thousand men if Evans's brigade had returned from North Carolina, and if not, five thousand men including his brigade. Three days later, Evans wrote to his wife on this subject:

> I have received orders to go to Vicksburg, Miss. but Genl. Beauregard has suspended the order until he can hear from the Secretary of War again. As my Brigade is the only troops on James Island, I hope he will succeed in his protest for your sake and I earnestly believe that Charleston will be taken if the Secretary moves five thousand more troops which is the order now given to Beauregard. . . . Is it not too bad to leave so soon? But I will console myself with the chance of promotion and a large command. The latter I will take out with me and after the Summer Campaign return to my little family, so you must cheer yourself with this prospect if the order comes for me to leave which I yet hope will not be issued.[2]

Governor M. L. Bonham of South Carolina, Beauregard, and other prominent citizens protested to Davis about stripping the coastal defenses of so many troops, but the president was convinced that the Federals did not have a large force in South Carolina and Beauregard could spare the troops. Beauregard, therefore, on May 12, ordered Evans's brigade and one additional regiment, about 2,700 men, to report to Pemberton in Mississippi. In a letter to his wife the following day, Evans commented, "I have just recd. the order to go to Jackson Miss. I will leave tomorrow or next day for Cokesbury. The President was determined to send my Brigade anyhow. And I am now busy making preparations to get off. I regret to leave as my back pains me a great deal and I will have a long trip which will be more fatiguing than a campaign. . . ."[3]

After staying with his family a few days, Evans left for Mississippi. He missed his transportation connections in Washington, Georgia, and was forced to stay overnight. He enjoyed his stay in the Georgia city, however, spending some of his time conversing with Robert Toombs. On the morning of the twenty-fourth, Evans arrived in Montgomery, Alabama, where he joined his staff. Evans and his staff left that night for Jackson, Mississippi.[4]

Evans's men, however, did not follow their commanding general immediately. The transfer West did not sit well with many in the brigade and they decided that if they were going to be sent to some far away western battlefield to die, then they were first going to see their families one more time. As the train carrying men of the 17th and 18th Regiments passed through Branchville, South Carolina, many took the opportunity to pay a visit home.

On May 20, 1863, the *Yorkville Enquirer* wrote that many of the men of "17th and 18th Regiments . . . are fully represented in our District at this time. They determined to pay a flying visit home, and seem to be enjoying it; though we have strong suspicions that in their hurry, furloughs were *forgotten*."[5]

The number of men taking a "flying visit home" was so great that the Confederate authorities determined they could not discipline them all, so the generals decided to give them furloughs, and essentially pardons, if they reported to their units in Columbia by May 30. On that day the men were assembled and started their trip to Jackson. In his diary, Smith Ketchen recorded the response of General Evans when the "furloughed" men returned to the brigade:

June 5 [1863]. We got to Jackson at six oclock p.m. and was marched through the city by Capt. McCreary to General Evans headquarters in the suburbs near the ayslum of the south. When we got to the general's quarters or opposite the house in a grove of trees we were halted. When Capt. McCreary reported in person to Gen'l Evans the Gen'l. then came out to where we were standing in line smiling and appeared to be in the best of humour; and made the remark "Well boys, you have come to see me." After which water was brought to the men and they were dismissed to return to their respective companies and regiments.[6]

The good mood that Evans seemed to be in according to Ketchen was also expressed in an earlier letter to Vic when he wrote from Jackson on May 29:

Genl. Johnston is here looking remarkably well and is busy organizing his army. I have not yet been assigned to any command but expect to have a Division before we leave for the fight which I think will take place in about ten days. Gen. W. H. T. Walker has been promoted to a Major Generalcy and Gist is in his Division, and now at Canton. Vicksburg is still safe and I think will be able to hold out against Grant's army. We have killed a great number of them already, estimated 30,000. My Brigade is in good spirits, more so than the Mississippians. We have about 30,000 men now and more are daily arriving from Genl. Bragg's army, which will soon increase our army 50,000 independent of our forces at Vicksburg. So you see we will be strong enough to drive the Yankees out of the State and if we do I am of the opinion the war will soon end. May God grant it. The people are delighted to see me out here and have treated me very kindly. I send you a transcript from one of the newspapers here. The Yankees destroyed nearly all the municipal buildings in the city and the R. Road for some distance on both sides of the town and then left much frightened. Their stragglers are still being brought in, who are tired of the war . . . . I feel confident I will have a good time in this campaign as I will exert all my energies to obtain success, as I feel the President has sent me here at the solicitation of the state. In fact Gov. Brown (my true friend) told me my arrival was a token of favor from the President. . . .[7]

By the first of June, Grant had practically surrounded Vicksburg. Johnston's army was separated from Grant's by the Big Black River, whose fords were heavily guarded by the Federals. To reach Pemberton, Johnston would have to drive the Federals from between the river and Vicksburg. Johnston spent most of June making his army mobile and obtaining necessary supplies. He also made repeated requests for reinforcements.

During this time, Evans wrote repeatedly to his wife. On June 3, he reported:

> We are still at Jackson busy organizing. . . . Vicksburg still holds out and I am convinced can not be taken until we are prepared to relieve it . . . . Genl. Johnston will advance as soon as all of his troops arrive but you may rest assured he will not march until he is strong enough to drive the enemy away out of Mississippi . . . . Much to my surprise and pleasure I met Alfred [Evans's brother] here a private in Genl. Breckenbridge's Division. I have not seen him before in ten years. I will try to better his position and have him transferred to my Brigade. . . .[8]

There were a number of South Carolinians who migrated to Mississippi before the war. Evans met some old friends of his family near Jackson, about whom he wrote: "I find out here a large number of people from Marion. Tell Aunt Turpin her old friend Charlotte Greaves now Mrs. Stokes is looking very well. All the family are immensely wealthy. Jno. M. Greaves her old beau is worth a million of money and his brothers proportionately rich . . . ."[9]

In a letter dated June 13, Evans spoke of entertainment as well as war news:

> We are still awaiting orders and do not know when we will advance. The Yankees made a grand charge on Vicksburg last Tuesday with their whole force and were gallantly repulsed. We have slain at least 20,000 of them according to their own accounts. Truly has Vicksburg been the most sanguinary battle of the war so far. I hope we will be able to relieve the Garrison in a few days . . .
>
> My staff is now very full and I have a quite a number of

applications from my old Mississippi Brigade for positions which I am unable to give. Genl. French has arrived here but as yet has no command. I think Genl. Johnston is at a loss what to do with him as Johnston has no confidence in his capacity. . . . I have only two sweethearts whom I think are the authors of the occasional puffs of myself that are seen in the Jackson newspapers. They are very interesting young ladies and seem so anxious about my comfort, if I sleep well, if my clothes are mended, and if I have good things to eat. They sing and play for me every evening. Don't you think your husband is lucky to have such good ministering angels around him who look so fresh and cool in the morning as they greet him with the welcome smile at breakfast . . . I showed them your likeness and they admired it very much . . . .[10]

In a letter written June 17, Evans told of an interview with some old friends and of a very generous offer made to him:

My old St. Louis friends came to see me yesterday and are anxious that I should be ordered to Missouri with Genl. Price. My old friend Mrs. Choceteau thinking I wanted money sent me a check for twenty thousand dollars which she wished me to use as long as I wished. I declined her kind offer but told her son should I resign I would accept her very kind offer. Mrs. Choceteau also sent me a silver medal to wear around my neck to keep the Devil and Yankee bullets away. I will wear the medal tho' I am not a Catholic. . . .[11]

As the days passed, Evans was still confident that Vicksburg would be relieved:

Heavy firing is now being heard from Vicksburg, but we do not feel at all uneasy as to the result. The enemy has not fired a gun for the last five days until this morning. Genl. Gardner has repulsed Banks at Port Hudson and Kirby Smith (Seminole) is certainly at Millikins Bend and will be able to retard reinforcements and supplies to Grant's Army. Genl. Price is also again in the field. *We* are now awaiting for something to *turn up* so we can move. We are all ready fully equipped and in fine spirits. Genl. Johnston is determined to be safe when he attacks. The eyes of the world both Yankee and Confederate are now watching his movements. I never saw my Brigade more anxious for a fight. All the people out here look upon us as their protectors and openly say they have never seen gentlemen soldiers before. We are so modest and well behaved. (so much for having such a good General you will say) I can not say when we will move as everything will have to be *fully ripe* before we commence plucking!! I was sorry to hear of Frank Hampton's death in Va. but I confess I am not surprised when Stuart commands. He has never yet won a battle, and his conduct in this one should be and is condemned by every military man . . . . I see that McMaster is acquitted and the Court blames me for preferring changes against such a _____ rascal. I have published him in orders as released from arrest with the remarks that the Court seemed more moved by sympathy for the accused than any sense of moral obligation or interest of his services. I will again arrest him when he returns. . . .[12]

Johnston must have found a command for French, because on June 23, Evans's brigade was assigned to French's division. The brigade had previously served in William W. Loring's and John C. Breckinridge's division since its arrival in Mississippi. A day later, Evans wrote:

We left Jackson on the 22nd. and are now about the same distance from Vicksburg whence we are now in hearing of heavy cannonading. Our troops still hold out nobly and I do pray Heaven may continue until we can relieve them. I am now under Genl. French who has a Division of three brigades. I am the senior Brigadier and will have everything pretty much my own way for I am certainly a better General than French. Genl. Johnston is truly unfortunate in Divisional Commanders. Loring, French, and Walker, neither of whom can manage an Army. We have rendezvoused here for what reason I am unable to say, but I expect it is a strategic move of Johnston. We will probably advance in a day or two. I wish it were tomorrow for we are all now ready . . . Oh how I wish I could relieve our brave comrades. I have all my staff with me and am now in the midst of my rich kin who send me nice vegetables, mutton and butter. Asa is now on a visit to them. I could not leave camp . . . . I do not apprehend any severe fighting by our Division. We will trust more to strategy than to actual engagements as we are too weak to offer them battle direct . . . .[13]

During the inactivity of Johnston's army, Evans visited his relatives. In a letter written June 28, he discussed his visit and the latest war news:

> I have just returned from my cousin Mary Greaves where I spent two days very pleasantly. I have any number of pretty cousins who treat me very affectionately and say how they wish I was not married as they know I am a good husband. That I would be such a fine catch for the girls. I rode out on horseback with Mary Greaves yesterday. The first time I have committed such an offense since I was married. I brought the whole family to church to hear our Chaplain Mr. Giredeau of the 23rd., so you see I am in good hands. Vicksburg still holds but no firing heard for the last two days. I think the Yankees are getting tired. I am unable to say when we will move. We are still collecting troops preparatory to some demonstration. Genl. Johnston however keeps his counsel so no one knows what we are to do . . . . I expect that you will hear that I was under arrest.[14] Genl. Johnston arrested me on a point of military etiquette but released me next day with his regrets. The question was about official channels in which I differed with the General. The matter is now settled decidedly in my favor.
>
> I received a letter from Mart yesterday. He says my move to the West has benefitted me in the Department in Richmond. That everyone speaks of the military importance of my presence out here. I think I will be kept out here now and do not expect to return to Carolina (except on leave of absence) until the war is over, I will try to see you in October, should it please Heaven to spare my life . . . .[15]

The following day, Johnston ordered his command to advance toward the Big Black River. He had no idea of trying to raise the siege, but hoped to extricate Pemberton and his garrison. Evans seemed confident that they would be successful, as he wrote on July 2:

We are now marching on Vicksburg to relieve if possible the noble little Garrison who still holds out. I think we will not have much difficulty in getting in as Smith (Seminole) has cut off his supplies. We will probably have some skirmishing in a day or two probably a fight. I have every confidence in our success. I hope to be able to write my next letter from Vicksburg. . . .[16]

Evans's dispute with McMaster continued. Evans wrote: "Tell Frank [Gary] to look out for McMaster papers in the Columbia newspapers. I have arrested him again. The scoundrel feels aggrieved at my orders in his case and has written an insulting paper to me. I think I have him now and will certainly keep him so . . . ."[17]

On July 4, Pemberton surrendered to Grant, but the news had not reached Johnston's army. On the same day, Evans was as confident as ever that Vicksburg would be saved:

Vicksburg holds out nobly. The enemy are not as strong as we supposed and are getting sick numbers dying daily. We are now only four miles from them and all of us anxious for the order to advance. We now hear the cannon distinctly, while all is quiet in our camp not a drum heard or a bugle sounded. . . .Genl. Gist is encamped near me in fact all of Genl. Johnston's Army is here in excellent spirits and health. The Genl. however is very cautious and is studying the position of the enemy. . . .[18]

That night Johnston received news of the fall of Vicksburg. After learning this, he gave orders for his army to retreat to Jackson, which it reached on the afternoon of the seventh. Two days later, General William T. Sherman appeared before Jackson with a large Federal force and began to construct batteries. During the next several days there was constant skirmishing between the opposing armies, and the Federal batteries shelled the city incessantly. On the fourteenth, Evans wrote:

This is the 5th. day we have been skirmishing. No general attack has yet been made. Grant with one Division made an attempt to turn our left flank but was easily repulsed by Breckenridge. We captured two or three hundred prisoners and killed quite a number. My loss is small yet not more than fifty altogether. . . .[19]

The next day, Evans related the latest developments: "The Battle still continues. I have lost very few. The enemy are very strong and I fear we will be obliged to fall back to secure our R Road communication open . . . .We are all in good spirits and health . . . . I eat only once a day, cold meat and bread. The enemy are trying to shell us from our position. Bombs are bursting all around me. My courier Kinlock was shot by my side yesterday but is going well . . . ."[20]

On the night of the sixteenth, Johnston withdrew from Jackson. He was able to save not only his army, but also his supplies, wagon trains, and artillery. The Confederates continued to fall back until they reached Morton, Mississippi, on the twentieth. The Federals sent a small force in pursuit, which contented itself with destroying the communication lines. Evans, disgusted by the Confederate retreat, wrote home very critical of it:

> We have now fallen back to this place thirty miles from Jackson where we left last Thursday night. The enemy did not follow us till the day after we left. He is now however reported as being twenty miles in our rear, but I think it is only a cavalry force catching stragglers. I am glad we have left the trenches about Jackson as my Brigade suffered both from disease and the enemy without much chance to engage the enemy. I have lost one hundred and eleven killed & wounded but very few killed, a great many slightly wounded. Our policy seems to be to fall back until we are reinforced which God grant may be soon as I am heartily sick of retreating which is very demoralizing to our troops. Oh how I wish I was back in Virginia with a victorious army. I am fearful my Brigade will be contaminated by this Western atmosphere of falling back, maneuvering and retreating. I can see no chance of distinction or promotion out here and as my relatives have all been either taken or run off by the Yankees, I do not care how soon I am ordered back either to South Carolina or Virginia. . . .[21]

Several days later, Evans wrote to his wife expressing his anxiety over the safety of Charleston and again of his desire to return to South Carolina in order that he might help defend his native state:

We have just stopped to let our supply train of three hundred wagons pass. Will probably be ordered today again toward Meridian . . . . I wish I could return to Charleston immediately, but I am convinced I am out west for the war, and will be compelled to ask for a leave of absence to visit my little family . . . . I am very anxious about Charleston and I think Genl. Beauregard should charge the enemy at once even if it cost dearly and drive him off Morris Island for as long as he has a footing he can annoy us. I am glad that Frank went because every man who does not turn out now, should be branded a traitor. Certainly the prospect before us requires the energy and immediate action of everyone capable of bearing arms . . . .[22]

After pillaging and burning Brandon and Jackson, Sherman evacuated the latter on the twenty-third and returned to Vicksburg. Evans's brigade remained near Morton, and at the end of July he wrote:

I am proud to see John [Gary] is going good . . . with his Battery. . . .The Yankees all have left us out here and probably gone to Tennessee and towards Mobile. We are daily expecting some of them to turn up. Where we will either be ordered to Mobile or to help Genl. Bragg in North Alabama and Georgia. All of us here are disgusted with Genl. Lee's operations. He has nearly ruined us by going on his wild goose chase into Maryland and Penn. We will require two or three months to recover from the disaster. I am however cheerful and full of confidence in our noble and sacred cause and would sacrifice myself and family before I would beg for peace or make one offer for conciliation.[23]

On August 2, General Samuel Cooper notified Johnston to send Evans's brigade to Savannah immediately, but for Johnston to keep the horses and artillery of the brigade for the time being. The following day, Johnston instructed Evans to proceed with his brigade to Savannah.[24] Evans arrived in Savannah six days later and wrote to his wife soon afterward:

My Brigade was ordered to this place (much to my joy) by the President himself for what reason I have no idea. I expect some of my troops this afternoon and think that the whole

Brigade will arrive by tomorrow night. I have telegraphed Genl. Beauregard for instructions, in the meantime I will put my Brigade in Camp about seven miles out to be in a healthy location . . . . I think I will be held in reserve near Charleston which would suit me . . . .[25]

With the arrival of Evans in Savannah, there arose the question of who would command the District of Georgia, which formed a part of the Department of South Carolina, Georgia, and Florida under the command of Beauregard. If Evans remained stationed at Savannah, he would automatically succeed Brigadier-General H. W. Mercer, who was Evans's junior in rank. Upon hearing of Evans's assignment to Savannah, on August 5 Mercer wrote Thomas Jordan, Beauregard's chief of staff, that he would cheerfully relinquish the post to Evans, but he hoped that Evans would continue the work he had started. Two days later, Beauregard instructed Mercer to continue in command; Evans's brigade would be held in reserve.[26]

On August 8, Beauregard wired Cooper: "If Evans's brigade is sent to Savannah, he will command General Mercer, which ought not to be." Cooper replied the same day: "You can make such disposition of Evans's brigade as you may deem best. It was sent to Savannah on your request for troops at that place. If it remains there, rank must have its effect . . . ." Upon receiving this communication Jordan wired Evans: "Hold your brigade in reserve, ready for emergency, not assuming command of the District of Georgia. Send me return."[27]

Several days later, the Federals made an attack upon Battery Wagner in Charleston Harbor. Captain John Hillary Gary, Evans's brother-in-law, was in command of Company A of Lucas's battalion stationed at this battery. On the eleventh, Sergeant T. H. Tynes of Gary's command fell mortally wounded. As Evans learned of the events: "Capt. John H. Gary, seeing his gallant sergeant fall, went at once to him, and was overcome by the sight of his terrible wound. 'I am dying, Captain, but I am glad it is me, and not you.' Devoted to his sergeant, Gary burst into tears, when Tynes gasped, almost with his last breath, 'I can be spared: but our country can't spare you, Captain.'"[28]

Two nights later, Gary himself was severely wounded. Upon hearing of the seriousness of Gary's wound, Evans left immediately for Charleston, arriving there on the fourteenth. He stayed at his brother-in-law's bedside until young Gary passed away early on the morning of the seventeenth. Bishop Capers eulogized Gary as "an accomplished young officer, of the highest promise, beloved and honored by his command, and distinguished for his personal gallantry." Heartbroken by his death, Evans returned to Savannah.[29]

On August 25, Beauregard ordered Evans to report to Charleston with four regiments, leaving his strongest regiment for the present in Savannah. The following day Evans wrote his wife: "I have just recd. orders to go to Charleston and will leave in the morning I suppose again to be held in reserve . . . . I enclose you a beautiful tribute to our beloved John. The last sentence is mine. I was sent for to give his history. Paste this transcript in my bible as Woodson's and Andrew's are. . . .Tell all the people not to be afraid of Charleston falling. The Yankees can shell it for two years without doing much injury. . . ."[30]

Evans finally was back home in Charleston as he had long wished. However, events would soon unfold quite unlike he had anticipated.

— Chapter X —

CHARLESTON COURT-MARTIAL

S oon after his arrival in Charleston, Evans assumed command of the 2nd Sub-Division of the First Military District, which was under the command of Brigadier-General Roswell S. Ripley. On August 27, Thomas Jordan notified Ripley that Evans's brigade had been assigned to his district. He stated to Ripley that since the brigade had been ordered to Christ's Parish, it should be employed in clearing the trees for a mile and a half in front of the lines, so that the Confederates could better resist a Federal advance in that direction. Jordan also instructed Ripley to see that the brigade was in proper position to act as a support to the garrison on Sullivan's Island if an emergency arose.[1]

Several weeks later, Evans received the following orders from Ripley:

1st. That you will take your Hd. Qurs. on Sullivans Island.
2nd. That Genl. Clingman's Command will be confined to his own Brigade, giving his special attention to the State of discipline and its general condition.
3rd. That Col. Anderson who will report to you for duty to be placed in command of the outposts, will report directly to you.

4th. That Col. Keitt will be placed in command of his
Regiment as soon as he has completed certain important
special service.[2]

Evans and Ripley met shortly thereafter. A careful reading of the
documents suggests that this interview must have been stormy.
Apparently, Ripley was offended by something Evans said and
wrote Evans the next day:

I have the honor to enclose herewith copies of certain communications & orders sent to you from these Head Quarters since
the 7th. of September. The execution of some of the provisions
contained therein were verbally permitted to be delayed at your
interview yesterday.

A consideration of the orders, however, has shown that it is
necessary for the public service that every provision shall be carried out *immediately* and you will execute them without delay. . . .

Hereafter it is to be understood that no departure or delay in
executing orders in any way be countenanced or permitted.[3]

Evans resented this and took it as a reprimand. He returned the
letter with the following endorsement: "Respectfully returned. I
cannot admit of any reprimand from the Brig. Genl. Commdg."
But then went on:

You can scarcely imagine my surprise at the tenor of your letter of this date. I had flattered myself that you were sufficiently
conversant with my military antecedents to prohibit such a letter
that you have written today. I think I have proved on several battle fields my obedience to the orders of my superiors. Also my
duty to my country, in using all personal exertions to get the
advantage of the enemy. Your letter leaves me but little discretion, and I cannot imagine that you have forgotten the known
military maxim 'that every good soldier will use every effort to
attain success to his command.' In conclusion I would add that I
feel myself competent to execute any order that you may give, as
well as to give the enemy some evidence of the presence of my
Brigade. The orders emanating from your office have been, or are
now being executed.[4]

Evans did not let the matter drop. Two days later he wrote Jordan requesting that he and his brigade "be relieved from duty under the command of Brig. Genl. R. S. Ripley. I would remind the General that Brig. Genl. Ripley is the only senior I have in the Department."[5]

Much to Evans's surprise, the following order from Captain W. F. Nance, assistant adjutant-general, was presented to him in response:

> The Brig. Genl. Comd'g. directs that you [W. Gordon McCabe] proceed to Mount Pleasant or Sullivans Island wherever Brig. Genl. Evans may be found and order him in arrest at the house he occupies on Mt. Pleasant with his limits one mile around. You will direct Brig. Genl. Evans to transfer the command of the 2nd Sub-Division at once to Brig. Genl. Clingman, with all the orders, letters and other papers of instruction he may have received.
>
> You will also direct Genl. Evans to order his staff officers to report for immediate duty to the Senior Colonel of his Brigade during Brig. Genl. Evans' arrest.
>
> This order is positive and immediate.[6]

Evans wrote to Nance immediately, asking why he was arrested and, if charges were to be preferred against him, what they would be. His letter was returned the same day with this endorsement: "Respy returned. A copy of the charges will be furnished Genl. Evans when they are made. By command of Brig. Genl. Ripley."[7]

At the same time Evans wrote Jordan that he had received an order from Ripley placing him under arrest but had not been informed for what offense. He requested Jordan to suspend the charge since the enemy was in his front. Jordan returned the letter with his endorsement of the arrest, and Evans then applied to him for a reconsideration. Evans also wrote to Beauregard arguing that he had not committed a military misdemeanor that would warrant his arrest and appealed to Beauregard to suspend his arrest. Beauregard replied the next day:

> Your letter of the 20th. inst. Has just been recd. I regret not being able to comply with your request to have you released at

this moment when the Enemy is in our front. The charge against you is for disobedience of orders with 3 specifications, &, I regret to say, appears to be well founded- the nearer the Enemy the more attentive should officers & soldiers be in obeying orders. Your court will be ordered to assemble as soon as practicable.[8]

Still hoping that Beauregard would reconsider his case, Evans wrote him as soon as he received Beauregard's rejection of his first plea:

I deem it my duty as a patriot and a Carolinian and a soldier who has no aspirations save to do his duty, that these charges should be investigated at once. I know they must be frivolous & futile, the trial I also deem it my duty to solicit . . . .

In conclusion I would express my disappointment at your decision in my case, even if the charges were true, my suspension should be granted, especially by one so patriotic as yourself.

I am the only military educated man on the Island. My patriotism, devotion and capacity have been proven, and you well know my subordination.

I am constrained to believe that the charges preferred against me were not promoted by any patriotic motives.[9]

About the same time, Ripley sent Evans the charges he had preferred against him. Evans quickly acknowledged receipt of the charges and asked for a court to be called as soon as possible.[10]

On the twenty-fifth of September, Evans wrote Jordan that he had been under arrest for nine days and as yet the Department had not set a date for his trial. He stated further that he was aware of the regulations regarding trials, but felt that one should be called at a very early date, because his brigade needed his attention.[11]

Five days later, Evans was notified that his trial would be held in Charleston on October 2. He appeared confident of the outcome as he wrote his wife:

My trial will come off in a day or two. Everything looks favorable to me. My lawyers say my case is strong tho' I will have a strong party to content with. Col. Moses and Mr. Wilson Mitchell are my counsels. They both discussed with me yesterday. There is no feeling of animosity between myself and Ripley although I have a contemptible opinion of him. You may rest assured he will never challenge me. He is too great a coward. Col. Moses tells me the whole Legislature is in my favor and would willingly come down to Charleston on my defence. On the whole I think the trial will benefit me anyhow in the state. . . .[12]

When the court convened on October 2, Ripley brought the following charges against Evans:

Charge
Disobedience of Orders

Specification 1st. In this that Brigadier General N. George Evans P.A.C.S. having received orders on or about the 28th. of August 1863, from the Head Quarters of the 1st Military District in accordance with instructions from the Head Quarters of the Department of South Carolina, Georgia and Florida, to cause his Brigade to be employed in placing the lines in Christ Church Parish, S.C. in a proper condition to resist an advance in that direction, and especially in cleaning away all timber in front of those lines for a distance of a mile and a half, did substantially fail to obey and carry out such orders. This within the limits of the 2nd. Sub-Division 1st. Military District, Department of So. Ca. Georgia and Florida, and between the 28th day of August and the 15th day of September 1863.

Specification 2nd. In this that Brig. Genl. N. George Evans P.A.C.S. having received directions from the Head Quarters of the 1st Military District, Dept. So. Ca.. Ga. & Fla. Dated Sept. 9th 1863 to take his Hd. Grs. on Sullivan's Island, said directions having been reiterated on the 12th. day of September 1863, did fail and neglect to obey such directions. This within the limits of the 2d. Sub-Division 1st Military District, Dept. So. Ca. Ga. & Fla. and between the 9th. day and the 15th of September 1863.

Specification 3d. In this that Brig. Genl. N. George Evans P.A.C.S. having received instructions from the Hd. Qrs. of the 1st Military District, Dept. So. Ca. Ga. And Fla., on or about the10th of September 1863 which instructions were repeated on the 12th of September 1863 to furnish facilities to Col. L. M. Keitt 20th S.C. Volunteers on special duty of collecting boats and water transportation in Christ Church Parish did fail and refuse to obey such instructions. This within the limits of the 2d. Sub-Division of the 1st Military District of the Department of So. Ca. Ga. & Fla., and at different times between the 10th and 14th of September 1863.[13]

It took the court approximately two weeks to examine all the witnesses in Evans's case. To his credit Evans succeeded in providing sufficient testimony to refute all the charges of disobedience. In answer to the first specification, Evans produced witnesses who stated that he had detailed men to clear the timber and build the needed fortifications, but these men were hindered in their work because the Department had not furnished them the necessary tools. In answer to the second specification it was by competent testimony that Evans had selected a house on Sullivan's Island and had declared his intention to live there. Evans answered the last specification by proving that he had detailed thirty men to assist Keitt with his work, exactly the number of men Keitt had requested.[14]

Evans appeared confident that he would be acquitted when he wrote his wife on October 12 that

> The prosecution in my case have proven nothing of any importance so I am convinced that I will be fully acquitted and sustained in my course. My counsel thinks the Court will reprimand Ripley. I have a great many friends and a few bitter enemies. McMaster's faction who seem glad to see me tried. My Brigade sustained me as they know it was a Brigade quarrel. . . . My Court will be over tomorrow and as soon as I am released I will apply to go home. I cannot promise you that I will succeed as Ripley will doubtless be prejudiced more after the trial is over . . . .[15]

At this time, Evans was anxious to be in Cokesbury with his wife, who was expecting the birth of their child. He was not released by the court in time, however, to return home. On October 17, he received word from Cokesbury that two days earlier his wife had given birth to another son. This baby boy, who was destined to become South Carolina's youngest governor, was named John Gary after the gallant captain of Battery Wagner. Evans wrote his wife immediately: "You cannot imagine the relief to my anxious heart and further to learn you and your babe were doing well. Truly has God blessed us. I was in ectacies when I heard my dear dear wife was doing well. Oh! How I wish I were with my dear wife to watch her and administer to her every want. . . ."[16]

An incident occurred on November 2, which no doubt brought much happiness to Evans and raised his spirits even as he was under arrest. That night he was serenaded by the Virginians of Brigadier-General Henry A. Wise's brigade. After the serenade, several officers called upon Evans and requested him to address the Virginia troops, a number of whom had served under him at Leesburg. From the portico of the Charleston Hotel, Wise introduced Evans to the Virginians. Evans stated that he greatly appreciated their compliment and that it "excited his warmest emotions." He explained further that he had witnessed the gallantry of the Virginians on their native soil, but after seeing their cheerfulness and anxiety to meet the foe who was now threatening Charleston, he was sure that they were patriots indeed. He again expressed his appreciation for the serenade and then retired.[17]

Jefferson Davis was in Charleston at this time and Evans visited him the following night, making an appointment for the next morning. Evans wrote his wife about the interview: "This morning I had a private interview with him [Davis] and he wrote Beauregard about my case. I told the President that I truly considered myself imposed on and requested his protection. My trial has not been published, but I expect it will be in a day or two . . . ."[18]

On the following day G. W. C. Lee brought welcome news to Evans when he wrote, "I made inquiries yesterday by direction of the President in regard to your case. I was informed that you had been acquitted by the Court, and that there had been some delay in reviewing the proceedings, but that the orders in the case would be published in a day or two. We are off in a moment for Wilmington."[19]

Evans then wrote Lee that the proceedings had not been published, although "they had been in the hands of the reviewing authority twenty-two days."[20] Immediately, Evans wrote his wife of the latest developments:

I received a letter from my brother Tom yesterday from Marion. He went to see the President as he passed. The President told him he approved my course and had *no doubt* 'my trial would result in my promotion. That one thing was certain Col. Keitt would never have the commission of Brigadier General.' I have again called the attention of the President to Beauregard's persecution which I think will secure my promotion. I have been acquitted by the Court of every specification, yet after *twenty five days reviewing* Beauregard will not publish the proceedings – the Gens. composing the Court are more anxious than myself, probably the Court has cast some censure on the Department is the reason the proceedings in my case have been delayed . . . .[21]

In the meantime, Evans had written to General George E. Pickett to ask for his brigade. Pickett answered promptly: "Yours of the 14th inst. Has just been received. I should like exceedingly to get your brigade & personal services in this Dept. and if you will forward immediately an official application to that effect, I will do every endeavor to effect it. In the meantime I will feel the pulse of the Department on the subject. . . ."[22]

Beauregard, however, had not published the court-martial papers. Frustrated by this, Evans bitterly denounced Beauregard in a letter home:

I am still awaiting orders from Beauregard, who seems to have been much enraged at the reception the President gave me. I hope I will be ordered to North Carolina where I would be free from this corrupt atmosphere and where I think I can be of more service. I am now still more convinced that the delay in publishing my acquittal is in order to give Col. Keitt command of the Brigade. I have again called the attention of the President to Beauregard's course. He has taken a month to review the proceedings in my case and no doubt would take a year, if he could . . . This Department is the most corrupt in which I have ever served . . . .[23]

Yet, Beauregard still refused to publish the orders releasing Evans from arrest. By late November, Evans wrote to Jordan requesting that the proceedings of the court be released. As usual, Beauregard and his staff remained silent and ignored Evans's letter. After waiting two days, Evans filed charges against Beauregard through the Department of South Carolina, Georgia, and Florida, of which Beauregard was the commander. Evans, fearing that Beauregard would not send the papers to Richmond, sent a duplicate to the War Department two days later. Evans brought the following charges against Beauregard: first, that he (Evans) had been under arrest since September 15, and although acquitted of the charges brought against him, Beauregard had refused to publish the papers releasing him from arrest. Second, that during his arrest, Beauregard had sent his inspector general to visit the officers and men of Evans's brigade for the purpose of asking his (Evans) inferiors in rank personal questions concerning his character as a gentleman and soldier. Evans further charged that this practice was unfair and would incite mutinous conduct within the brigade. Finally, that Beauregard had divided Evans's brigade into four detachments and had sent them into different military districts, thereby destroying the brigade organization. Evans added that this was not demanded by the exigencies of the service and was calculated to ruin the effectiveness of the brigade.[24]

On December 5, Cooper referred Evans's charges to Beauregard. Eleven days later, Beauregard answered the charges in a letter to Davis stating that he was delayed in publishing the orders of the case because of pressing military business "more important to the defence of this city, than . . . . Evans' return to the brigade . . . . and also, for about a month, from inability to have the order printed." Beauregard also asserted that the inspection was made by the department because of numerous reports concerning the bad discipline and low morale of the brigade. Too, Beauregard maintained that the regiments were transferred to different places because it was best for the defense of Charleston. Beauregard then stated that if Evans returned to the brigade, he would lower its efficiency; especially so, because of the relations existing between Evans and some of the commanders of the regiments of the brigade. Beauregard concluded by recommending that Evans be transferred to another department, since he had no confidence in Evans's ability.[25]

Evans, not hearing anything from his case, wrote to Samuel Cooper on December 27, requesting that his complaints against Beauregard be entertained and the verdict of the court-martial be published. Cooper then turned over all the proceedings in the case to Davis. Cooper also recommended to Davis that Evans be brought before an examining board in order to remove the disqualifications that Beauregard had placed against him and that Evans should be immediately released from arrest. Davis approved Cooper's recommendation on January 13, 1864.[26]

A few days later, Cooper wrote Beauregard that he must immediately release Evans from arrest and publish the final orders of his trial. He stated further that the president thought it would be unjust to transfer Evans to another department until he could acquit himself of the disqualifications Beauregard had brought against him.[27]

Beauregard soon replied that he had already published the proceedings of the trial and that Evans had been released from arrest on the seventeenth. He stated that the reason he had not already called the board of examiners was the inability to appoint a board and "my indisposition to subject an officer who had twice served in battle under my orders in the first year of the war with merit, indeed distinction, to humiliation involved by such an examination." Beauregard ended by declaring that he was satisfied that Evans would be detrimental to the brigade if returned to its command, so he would be compelled to call a board of examiners.[28]

After publishing the orders and releasing Evans from arrest, Beauregard did not return him to the command of his brigade. It is apparent that politics and intrigues behind the scene, not of any public record, played a part in Evans's troubles.

From the time of Evans's arrival in Savannah in August 1863, it seems that Beauregard disliked him. When he finally assigned Evans to a command, he placed him in the only district where Evans would not have been the superior officer. Indeed, Ripley was the only brigadier in the department who was senior in rank to Evans. If Beauregard considered Evans incompetent at this time, why did he not make charges against him then? Beauregard was possibly uncertain as to the outcome of any such charges and may have feared the effect of countercharges by Evans.

In reviewing Ripley's charges against Evans, it is evident that Beauregard acted firmly in upholding Ripley. If Beauregard had been as thorough in investigating these charges as he was later about the complaints concerning the conduct of Evans's brigade, he would no doubt have discovered that the charges against Evans would not hold up in court. But was he eager to find this out? From Beauregard's later actions, he apparently was quite happy to have the opportunity to silence Evans.

Beauregard's explanation — that he was too busy to issue the decision of the court-martial — is simply too contrived. It need have taken no more time than did writing out his reasons for inaction. Yet, he still did not want to face a board of examiners or to prefer charges against Evans. The intervention of Davis and the necessity of publishing the orders were obviously uncomfortable to Beauregard.

Although there had been previous reports about discontent in Evans's brigade, they were not as serious as Beauregard alleged. Why did Beauregard wait until Evans had been under arrest for over a month before he had the inspection made? The evidence reveals that it was Beauregard's intention to hurt Evans when he could the most.

Alfred Roman, who inspected the brigade for Beauregard, stated that there was considerable ill-feeling among the men and officers of the brigade against Evans. The extent of Colonel McMaster's responsibility for this may only be conjectured, but it was natural for McMaster to start his complaints in the brigade. He had been criticizing Evans ever since the regiment was stationed at Kinston.

The whole episode seems to boil down to this: Beauregard thought that the best way to deal with Evans was to keep him from his command; in essence, to refuse to permit Evans to join his brigade. Beauregard did not want to face the board of examiners, and it is hard to believe he postponed the calling of the board solely because of Evans's past services under him. He was probably aware that Evans would be cleared and realized that this would not place his action in a favorable light.

Ironically, Beauregard stated that he did not want to subject Evans to the examination by the board because Evans had previously served with such distinction under him. Is it possible that Beauregard recalled that Evans had certainly twice disobeyed orders and regarded those occasions with mixed emotions for personal reasons? The earlier orders which had been disobeyed had been Beauregard's, but there was no possibility then of bringing charges on either occasion. The first disobedience had saved a battle; the second had won a great victory. If Evans had not taken his stand at Manassas, Beauregard probably would have been forgotten on the field. Instead, Beauregard received the glory and barely mentioned the part Evans played in the battle. And Leesburg was too great a victory to censure Evans. Beauregard knew all of this, and apparently waited to retaliate until 1863, when he could keep Evans under arrest for months for charges that were unfounded.

The matter was taken out of Beauregard's hands on March 11, 1864, when James A. Seddon, secretary of war, issued the following orders: "Brig. Gen. N. G. Evans, Provisional Army, C. S. will forthwith proceed to take command of his brigade in the Department of South Carolina, Georgia and Florida."[29]

Evans reported for duty soon afterward and jubilantly wrote his wife:

> I received today my orders to take command of the two Regiments of my Brigade and Battery now here. The other Regiments will probably be ordered to me soon. I will move my Hd. Qrs. to Sullivan Island, but will keep up my horses at this place in order to keep my horses out of the range of the shells . . . The enemy are still shelling the City tho' without much effect. My Brigade is delighted at my return and several officers have visited me to welcome me back. My communication to Jordan reporting for duty fell like a bombshell amongst Beauregard's staff . . . .[30]

As soon as Evans reported to Jordan, the latter notified Beauregard. Beauregard instructed Jordan to place Evans on duty, but to have his case investigated by Generals Daniel H. Hill, Jeremy F. Gilmer, and James H. Trapier, as provided by law.[31]

Much to his chagrin, on April 6 Evans was assigned to command the 3rd-Sub-Division, which was in the First Military

District commanded once again by Ripley.[32] Evans did not like this arrangement. "I have applied to be sent in the field, either to Virginia or Georgia," he wrote his wife. "I am determined to get rid of Beauregard and Ripley and will continue to apply until I am ordered away."[33]

Evans's opportunity came sooner than he expected. On April 14, General Cooper instructed Beauregard to send Evans's brigade to Wilmington immediately. Accordingly, Beauregard ordered Evans to proceed at once with the infantry of his brigade to the North Carolina coast.[34]

Evans, however, never reached Wilmington. On the morning of the sixteenth, accompanied by A. L. Evans, he rode down Meeting Street in a light buggy drawn by two horses. They had passed the Charleston *Courier*'s office when one of the traces gave way which caused the horses to proceed at full speed. The sudden lurch by the horses broke the shaft and resulted in the front of the buggy falling to the ground. Evans, in trying to check the horses, was pulled over the dashboard and onto the pavement. His head struck the cobblestones with fearful violence. Several people from the *Courier* office ran to Evans's assistance and brought him into the office where a doctor was summoned immediately. Evans had suffered a severe blow where his head struck the stones. When picked up, he was unconscious and bleeding profusely from a lacerated wound on the right side of the head and from severe cuts about the eyes and mouth. His whole frontal bone was laid bare, all the skin being taken off. In a few minutes Drs. Lebry and Ogier, army surgeons, arrived and dressed the wounds. A little while later Evans was carried to the Schrimers's residence in Aiken Row, where he was examined by a Dr. Brodie.[35]

Evans's accident prevented him from leaving with his brigade and also meant that he would be unable to assume his duties for some time. In haste, Beauregard appointed W. S. Walker to take temporary command of the brigade.[36]

Evans's health problems only portended more bad times to come. His ongoing conflict with Colonel F. W. McMaster was about to erupt into open warfare, consuming much time and effort and preventing Evans from realizing any of his military goals and dreams.

Chapter XI

THE DISPUTE WITH McMASTER

Among many other reasons, Evans had been anxious to be released from arrest in order to settle a personal dispute with Colonel F. W. McMaster. The personal animosity between these two men had gradually grown more intense since the trial and vindication of Evans at Goldsboro the previous February. By spring 1863, McMaster had attempted to stir up trouble between Evans and Wade Hampton. After talking with McMaster, Hampton wrote Evans:

> In a recent conversation with Col. McMaster he accidentally used an expression which induced me to suppose that you had in his presence spoken in offensive terms of myself. After Col. McMaster had finished the discussion of the subject about which he was speaking, I recalled the expression he had used – which was that he "knew you were no friend to me" — & asked him what reason he had for saying this? He was unwilling to say anything farther on the subject. Regretted that he had made use of the expression referred to & requested me to let the matter drop. But upon my claiming it as a right that I should be informed of what you had said, he reluctantly repeated the substance of the

remarks made use of, though he did not recollect the precise language used. His statement was to the effect, that during a conversation in which mention was made of a fight that had occurred in Frederick City between my Brigade and the enemy, you after some disparaging remarks said "That you had in the presence of General Beauregard on the Battlefield of Manassas, a few days after the Battle there denied statements made by myself as to the position of my command during that fight; – That you had made me acknowledge that my statements were not correct; – That you had made me quail before you then; & that when you subsequently met me I seemed afraid & ashamed to look you in the face."

I avail myself of the first opportunity to call your attention to these statements of Col. McMaster as to the character of the language you held in reference to myself, in order that you may avow or disclaim the remarks which have been imputed to you.[1]

Very quickly, Evans responded to Hampton's letter and repudiated the accusations, "I have the honor to acknowledge the receipt of your letter of the 19th. Instant by the hands of Lt. Col. Green, and in answer beg leave to state that the remarks derogatory to yourself imputed to me by Col. F. W. McMaster are falsehoods."[2]

Hampton wrote different members of Evans's staff to see if the remarks were true. In response to Hampton, Major T. D. Eason wrote: "I received yours of the 18th yesterday, and in reply say that I have no recollection of ever having heard Genl. Evans make any remarks derogatory of you."[3]

McMaster continued to attack Evans whenever the opportunity presented itself. He even wrote and published a pamphlet about Evans. Then, at the trial of Major B. S. Bryan, he made several remarks injurious to Evans's character. Bearing these insults as long as he could, Evans wrote to McMaster: "The language affecting my reputation which you have thought proper to use in your testimony in the case of Maj. B. S. Bryan, and in a pamphlet purporting to be the proceedings of a Court Martial held at Wilmington No. Ca. Will receive proper notice at my hands as soon as my official relations towards you, and the duty which I owe to the Government will permit me."[4]

On March 2, 1864, Evans printed in the *Daily South Carolinian* the following correspondence pertaining to a proposed duel between Evans, A. L. Evans, and McMaster. Evans stated that the reason for the publication of the correspondence was to vindicate his character, which had been "assailed by Col. McMaster in print and in the official records of the country and in unmeasured private denunciations." Evans pointed out to the public that:

> McMaster in his correspondence with my brother, whilst making no allusion to his religious profession, assigns worldly reasons for declining a hostile meeting with him and indirectly invites an issue with myself. (It is proper to state that this correspondence took place without my knowledge.)
>
> In Col. McMaster's correspondence with myself his religious principles come into notice for the first time. The public must judge how far Col. McMaster's conduct towards me has been governed by Christian principles.[5]

On the same day that General Evans sent his note of warning to McMaster, the following letter from Captain Asa Lewis Evans was delivered to McMaster by Dr. P. P. Bonneau:

> The employment by you of certain offensive epithets, in relation to Brig. Gen. N. G. Evans, in a speech before a court martial, at Wilmington, N.C., came to my knowledge simultaneously with the report of your evidence in the case of Major B. S. Bryan, now undergoing investigation.
>
> This information I, for the first time, received on the 1st. instant, which sufficiently accounts for the delay of this communication.
>
> The gross and offensive aspersions of one to whom you owe obedience as your military commander – being made under cover of his disabilities – a regard alike for propriety and military discipline prelude him for noticing, and renders my right to reparation unquestioned as a member of his military family.
>
> These insults, when aimed at my chief, affect me, and I would be derelict both to the obligations to which my military relation binds me, as well as sense of personal honor assailed, were I, for a moment, to hesitate as to the propriety of this course.

My sense of injury is aggravated by the circumstance that you have taken occasion to promulgate the offensive expressions, in a pamphlet over your own signature, at a time when, even were you of equal rank, or belonging to a different command, imperative disabilities would raise obstacles to the proper treatment of them by Gen. Evans.

Inasmuch, then, that you have declared in substance in your published pamphlet, that the fact only of General Evans being your commanding officer has alone prevented you from seeking redress upon him, other than my public declamations, and because, as between myself and you, I conceive no impediment exists, I beg that you will, at your earliest convenience, afford to me an opportunity for satisfaction in the manner usual among men of honor.

Mr. friend, Dr. Bonneau, is authorized to arrange for me the necessary preliminaries.[6]

Failing to hear from McMaster in the allotted time, Bonneau wrote to him at Secessionville to ascertain whether he intended to reply to the letter. McMaster answered Bonneau's note stating that circumstances had prevented an earlier answer. He enclosed the following lengthy letter to A. L. Evans:

You remark that the employment of certain offensive epithets in relation to Brig. Gen. N. G. Evans, in a speech before a court martial, at Wilmington, N.C., came to your "knowledge simultaneously with a report of my evidence in the case of Major B. S. Bryan," the 1st. inst.

You again observe, that "the offensive aspersions of one to whom you owe obedience as your military commander, being made under cover of his disabilities, a regard alike for propriety and military discipline preclude him from noticing," &c.

You must excuse my dullness of comprehension in not being able to understand this sentence. If it means that the epithets in the pamphlet were made while the General was under arrest, it is a mistake, for they were used in a speech delivered in a public courthouse, 13th April, ult., before a general court martial, in the presence of about fifty members of the brigade – the majority from other regiments than my own. The publication of the pamphlet, it is true, did not occur until about a month ago. But you will observe from the preface, it was handed to the printer June 16th, ult.; ever since I have been urging it through the press. The "cover of disability" had nothing to do with it, and had the General been in full sway, with all his former power, it would have been promulgated as soon as it was issued.

If you mean my testimony was given during the General's arrest, I am sure I am not responsible for that, for I did not know what service I could be to Major Bryan when summoned, and was compelled as a witness to answer questions as to the best of my belief.

The implied censure in the phrase "to whom you owe obedience" I care nothing for. The matters of which you complain, occur in judicial proceedings. My speech is entirely supported by and logically deducible from the evidence in the case, and obedience to a military commander does not supercede the obligation to truth and justice.

The "cover of disability" seems to distress you. You next express your sense of injury at the time of the publication of my pamphlet "over my own signature at a time when even if" I "were of equal rank, or belonged to a different command, imperative disabilities would raise obstacles to the proper treatment of them by Gen. Evans."

This and "disabilities" again perplexes me, and I do not see how it throws the onus of resenting offensive aspersions on your soldiers. If it refers to the General's arrest, will the arrest be perpetual? If not, the disability will then be removed.

But the expression, "were you of equal rank," sounds quite harsh, from a captain to a colonel, challenging to mortal combat. For the colonel happens to be three grades above the captain and the general is only one removed from the colonel. If the disability is imperative in one instant, it is more imperative in the other.

You last state, that I have declared in substance, in my pamphlet, that General Evans being my immediate commanding officer, prevented me from obtaining redress other than by public declamations. This is a manifest mistake; there is nothing in my pamphlet to bear the construction you will impose on it.

Your right to reparation as a member of the General's military family may appear to you as a good reason, and may comport with the views of others. I appreciate the feeling when applied to a natural family. It would be exceedingly proper for a son to resent an injury inflicted upon a father, whose age, position in society, or sense of duty, might refrain from any violent measures. The reason, it strikes me, does not apply to a military family, which may be supposed to be composed of members, each of whom is able to take care of himself.

From the above reasons I do not see why you should undertake the difficulty of your General, and as I have no quarrel with you, I perceive no propriety in my have a personal conflict with you.

On account of these considerations, sir, and others, which I am under no obligations to mention to you, I respectfully decline making preliminary arrangements with Dr. Bonneau or any other friend you may select, for a hostile meeting with you . . . .[7]

Evans, under arrest at this time, could not have challenged McMaster. When he was told of his brother's letter, and McMaster's reply, he immediately sent the correspondence and the papers dealing with McMaster and himself to Messrs. W. W. Harlee, John S. Manning, and P. H. Nelson, who replied:

We are in receipt of all the papers committed to us in the matter between Col. McMaster and yourself and have carefully perused them.

It is our opinion that Capt. Evans had no right to make a personal demand upon Col. McMaster; and that matter is ended by the answer of Col. McMaster to his demand; and by having come to your knowledge.

At the same time we regard the evidence of Col. McMaster against you in the investigations in the case of Maj. B. S. Bryan Q.M. as vindicative and unnecessarily insulting.

We think therefore that it becomes you to vindicate your position in the matter, and do not think it necessary for you to resign for that purpose. Of course your commission will be thereby endangered; but that can only be regarded as one of the incidents growing out of an affair of so grave a character.[8]

Evans took the advice. Soon after he was released from arrest, he wrote to McMaster:

In conformity with my communication of November last, delivered to you by Lieut. S. J. Corrie, announcing that I would, at a proper time, take notice of your testimony in the case of Major B. S. Bryan, Quartermaster – as also of your pamphlet purporting to be a statement of the trial of yourself as an officer, and your defence thereon, in both of which you traduced in the most serious and remorseless manner, my conduct as an officer and my character as a man, I now demand the satisfaction due to a gentleman.

I have been delayed in making this call by being hitherto under official responsibility and military arrest.

My friend, Col. John Cunningham, who delivers this note to you, is authorized, on my part, to arrange and conduct the meeting.

The next day Cunningham delivered the note to McMaster who was stationed on Sullivan's Island. Upon receiving the note, McMaster stated that since his friend was sick, he would not be able to reply for some time. As Cunningham had to go to Richmond on business, he granted McMaster the courtesy of time. Cunningham returned to Charleston on the fifteenth and sent McMaster a note the next day asking for a reply to Evans's letter. McMaster answered immediately that he had been so busy with military matters that he had not had time to answer, but would do so in the next few days.

After waiting five days, Cunningham went to Green Pond, South Carolina, to see McMaster, but failed to find him. He then sent a note to McMaster asking for an immediate reply. McMaster responded to Cunningham with two notes. The personal note to Cunningham stated that circumstances delayed his answering earlier and requested Cunningham to deliver the other note to Evans. McMaster's answer to Evans was terse and defensive:

That you should have sent me an invitation to meet you in mortal combat, with a full knowledge of the fact that I am (to use your own language at Goldsboro) "a Ruling Elder in a Presbyterian Church," though not surprising to me, is wholly inconsistent with the position you aspire to occupy as a gentleman and a man of courage.

The only reply I deem necessary to your communication, is to repeat that of which you are already apprised, that I was born and educated a Presbyterian – a church which holds duelling to be a complex crime of both murder and suicide, neither of which I am prepared to commit.

In addition to this, I, as an officer in the Confederate army, have taken a solemn oath to observe the articles of war, by which duelling is positively forbidden, and as I regard an oath a sacred obligation, I do not desire to add perjury to the crime I would commit by accepting your challenge.

If further reasons were wanted, I might say that my life belongs to my country, in whose defence I have frequently heretofore exposed it and am ready to expose it again. But I am not prepared to throw it away in order to afford you an opportunity to establish a character for courage, which you have so many better opportunities of doing so in the cause of your country. You are welcome to such cheap reputation as you may make by challenging one whose whole life and character as a member of a Christian Church, gave you assurance that you could do so with impunity. But I must, at the same time, assure you that my religious scruples will not prevent me from defending both my person and my character in such manner as the laws of my country will sanction and all good men approve.[9]

John Cunningham appeared disgusted with McMaster, in a letter that he wrote to Evans:

A Christian's duty is not to offend or injure; but if he does, when he should be conscious of it, and refuses apology or reparation, he has saved or sacrificed all claim, or right of claim, to protection by his creed, or by his profession of it, wearing it as a *wolf does sheep's clothing*.

Col. McMaster does not lie in the above letter but tacitly admits your charge, that he attempted, in an outrageous manner, to traduce your conduct as an officer and your character as a man. He renders no excuse, no justification. His Christian professions neither prevented, not attempered, nor made reasonable, the persistent malignity of his attack.

Col. McMaster has declined to afford you suitable redress,

but says: "My religious scruples will not prevent me from defending both my person and my character in such manner as the laws of my country will sanction and all good men approve." He refuses to fight as a gentleman may fight, and as a gentleman should fight, in accordance with the high tone and conservative practice required and dictated by the Code of Honor and reason themselves; but he professes to be willing to fight in rencontre or melee. He accepts *that sort of duel,* but not the regulated and refined mode. He is willing, if I understand him aright to assassinate your body, as he attempted to assassinate your character.

Col. McMaster's allusion to the army regulations against duelling will be properly understood by all gentlemen and gentlemen officers. It would be "throwing pearls before swine" to controvert it.

His sending his reply, not through a gentleman or proper *friend,* and depending upon *my* courtesy for its delivery, was a "breach of decency" towards me, but which I *now* regard with *contempt.*

Let him go; he is not *worthy of your steel,* or the further notice of any gentleman.[10]

The publication of the correspondence ended the dispute between Evans and McMaster, but they remained personal enemies the rest of their lives.

— Chapter XII —

LAST DAYS

The feud with McMaster merely delayed the already lengthy time it took Evans to recover from his facial injury. While recuperating at home, he received a letter from his brother, Lieutenant-Colonel Beverly Daniel Evans, who was serving with Johnston's army near Atlanta. Eager to receive news of the war, Evans devoured the letter, which read in part:

> Last week I received a letter from Aunt Turpin, in answer to the one I wrote her making enquiries as to your condition, and was much gratified to learn from her that you were much improved and that now all the serious fears apprehended as to your safety mental and physical have entirely subsided and we indulge the hope that you will soon rejoin your command in the vigor of health and spirits . . . .
>
> I wrote you some time ago in reference to your difficulty etc. with McMaster. You have I think in popular estimation vindicated yourself handsomely and affixed the stigma of lying and falsehood upon your accusers. It is to be hoped the quietus your last card has given them will at least secure you from further annoyance from such unworthy sources.[1]

Although Evans was still ill, he went to Virginia in the early fall to resume his duties. He was not assigned to his brigade, however, so he remained in Petersburg waiting for orders. Early in October he wrote his wife:

> As I have quite recovered from my indisposition and am alone I will write you a few lines tho' I wrote you two days ago. I have not received my orders yet. My Brigade is very anxious for me to command them. This is Friday and if I do not receive instructions in two days more I will leave for Carolina and remain at home until my assignment. I am convinced Beauregard has done his best against me because I preferred charges against him. I almost wish they would retire me as they have done some half dozen Generals and let me get well at home . . . . I am in quite a fix. I am unwell and Isaiah Evans' slave sick. It is quite a labor for me to write . . . .[2]

It was some time before Evans received instructions to report for duty. On February 16, 1865, the War Department assigned him to the Department of South Carolina, Georgia, and Florida. As was to be expected, Evans did not like this assignment because it meant that Beauregard would once again be his superior officer. And because of unfavorable traveling conditions, he was unable to report to Beauregard until March 8.[3]

The day after Evans arrived, Beauregard ordered him to proceed to Goldsboro, North Carolina, and to report to General Johnston. At the same time, Beauregard wrote Johnston that he considered Evans incompetent to command and had so informed the War Department more than a year ago.[4]

Evans arrived in Raleigh on March 17 and immediately asked Johnston for instructions. Johnston replied several days later that there was not a command to which Evans could be assigned. Finally, at the end of March, Evans received orders from Johnston to return to South Carolina and there await instructions.

By this time, however, the collapse of the Confederacy was fast approaching. Lee withdrew from Richmond in early April and Davis began his trip to the lower South. After Lee surrendered at Appomattox Court House, Brigadier-General Mart Gary left with a detachment of his cavalry and cut his way through the Federal lines to join Davis's escort in North Carolina. Evans also united with the escort in that state; in fact, Davis and his cabinet were safely conducted to Cokesbury by these troops. The president stopped at the Gary home in Cokesbury on May 1, where he was given a big reception by Mrs. Thomas R. Gary, Evans's mother-in-law. He left early the next morning for Abbeville to hold the last meeting of his cabinet. After the meeting he traveled southward, but was soon captured in Georgia. Evans and Gary remained at Cokesbury.[5]

With the war's end, Evans went into the cotton business in Charleston. When the venture did not prove successful and was not compatible to his taste, he returned to Cokesbury, where he founded a small school. The school was too small for Evans though and in 1867 he heard of a principal's vacancy at Midway, Alabama. Toward this end, he wrote his old Abbeville friend, Dr. Lomax, who now resided in Midway, to assist him. The doctor being sick, Mrs. Lomax replied:

> You desire to know who is Chairman of the Board of Trustees of the Methodist School in Midway. Since the war there has been no trustees; the School is now under the supervision of Mr. Craven. Col. James Trenette was Chairman of the Board of Trustees before the war, and still takes more interest in the School than any one else – And will answer any questions – Besides, I believe he has more influence in relation to the school than any man in the place.
>
> There is no fixed salary, but the school itself will pay well. This session opens with 86 scholars. For the English Branches $30 in gold, the higher branches relatively high.
>
> I do not think you can purchase a house here, without paying very high for it, but I *think* your family can be boarded for $50 a month.[6]

The proposition appealed to Evans, so he went to Midway, "where I will have a more extensive field of prospects and can better support my family."

> Today the patrons of my school had a meeting, elected a Board of Trustees and arranged the matters of the school. They

have rented me a comfortable house with four rooms . . . a fine garden . . . The school is very promising and if you will teach the musical scholars and help me with the little scholars, I am convinced we will realize two thousand dollars the next year. . . . I will go right to work and furnish the home for your reception, so pack up and come on. Bring as much bedding as you can transport without much expense. I think it best to meet you in Columbus, if Billy or Mart will put you on the train in Augusta. You will have little trouble till you get to Columbus where I will meet you, and I will have a carriage to bring us from the depot to this place. Leave my desk and books until I get money for their transportation . . . .

Don't forget to ask Mr. Fleming for my check letter.[7]

Mrs. Evans left with her three sons for Alabama as soon as she received her husband's letter. Evans's third son had been born on September 15, 1865, and was named Barnard Bee in remembrance of that gallant soldier and life-long friend of Evans.

To help him launch the new school, Shanks asked his brother Beverly to write an introductory letter about him since "The people of Alabama and Georgia do not know me." Beverly's letter spoke of a new Nathan George Evans, not the hard-fighting, profane, and self-absorbed general perhaps others had known. Quite the contrary, in fact, the new Shanks was a hard praying, sincere, and humble member of the Methodist Church. "Thank God," Shanks wrote his brother Beverly, "he has opened my eyes and understanding to my situation and I have repented and am now trying to serve God."

On October 24, 1868, the Evanses had another child, a girl who was christened Mary Martin.[8] But General Evans did not live long after her birth. His old injury once again began to plague him, hastening his final illness. On November 28, 1868, at the age of forty-four, Shanks Evans died.

As soon as he heard of Evans's death, Mart Gary wrote his sister:

I have just learned of the death of Genl. Evans. I was not surprised as I have long thought that he would die suddenly. I deeply sympathize with you in your great loss, for he was a man of noble and generous character. I always have been fond of him, and sincerely regret his death. It will be impossible for me to come after you, owing to my business. Ma says you must come home and live with her. Brother Bill will leave here in a few days for you. You had better have everything in readiness. Your wishes as to the internment of the Genl's remains shall be carried out. I shall take great pleasure in extending all the care and protection of a brother to you and your children.

I have no words of comfort to write, as I know that nothing can compensate or alleviate the loss of a dear friend. The heart must be permitted to have its own course, tears, more tears are the greatest relief.[9]

General Evans's remains were brought back to Cokesbury for burial in the old cemetery. Soon after his death, it was discovered that Evans had five thousand dollars worth of insurance. This policy had been generously carried for several years by one of Evans's former soldiers, who was an insurance agent, after Evans had allowed the policy to lapse. The money was turned over to General Gary, who was the guardian for Shanks's children.

Mart Gary was devoted to his charges. He educated all of them in the secondary schools and then sent them to college. He did this out of his own funds and did not touch the legacy Evans had left. Indeed, he invested this money wisely and when General Gary died in 1881, the sum had increased to eighteen thousand dollars.

Shanks's children made impressive records in their native states. The three boys became outstanding lawyers, and one of them, John Gary, became governor of South Carolina in 1894. The general would have been particularly proud to know that during the Spanish-American War, Major John Gary Evans served on the staff of his old comrade, Fitzhugh Lee.

But, the military wars of Shanks Evans were over. The war with history, however, had just begun.

Notes

Chapter I

1. Morgan Edwards, "Materials Toward a History of the Baptists in Delaware State," Vol. [Part] III, in *Pennsylvania Magazine of History and Biography*, IX, (Philadelphia, 1885).
2. The disagreement came about as a result of a controversy over *laying-on-of-hands*. David Benedict, *General History of the Baptist Denomination in America*, II (Boston, 1813), 4–5.
3. Edwards, "Materials Toward a History of the Baptists in Delaware State," 48–50.
4. James Daniel Evans, *History of Nathaniel Evans and his Descendants* (Columbia, South Carolina, 1904), 2–7.
5. Edwards, "Materials Toward a History of the Baptists in Delaware State," 51–52.
6. Alexander Gregg, *History of the Old Cheraws* (Columbia, 1905), 47–49, quoting *Council Journal*, No. 7, 51–52.
7. Ibid., 49–50, quoting [South Carolina] *Gazette*, February 5–12, 1737.
8. Edwards, "Materials Toward a History of the Baptists in Delaware State," 51–52.
9. Gregg, *History of the Old Cheraws*, 75.
10. Evans, *Nathaniel Evans*, 13.
11. Gregg, *History of the Old Cheraws*, 59–60, quoting *Council Journal*, No. 7, 55–58.
12. As each grant of land was taken up by a settler, it was duly surveyed by the surveyor-general of the province or his deputies. The plots with full descriptions attached were then filed and recorded at Charles Town, the seat of government at the time. After this procedure had been complied with, the grantees usually presented their "Memorials" to the governor and His Majesty's Council, and if approved they were recorded in special books. Nathan (Nathaniel) Evans appears to have failed to memorialize his

187

first grants, but his later ones are to be found in Volumes 9 to 11 of Memorials, Secretary of State's Office, Columbia, South Carolina. Evans, *Nathaniel Evans,* 13–14.

13. No further information concerning his wife has been found.
14. Evans, *Nathaniel Evans,* 14–15.
15. Gregg, *History of the Old Cheraws,* 66–67.
16. Ibid., 109–112.
17. Ibid., 112–114, citing *Statutes at Large of South Carolina,* IX, 144.
18. It was published, however, by the *Gazette,* June 9–16, 1775.
19. Gregg, *History of the Old Cheraws,* 230–232.
20. Records in the Secretary of State's office in Columbia, South Carolina Indent No. 317, Book "O" show that Nathan Evans received compensation for his military services at various times after the war. On April 14, 1785, he received from the State of South Carolina 644 sterling for militia duty in 1778. Another record in Book "W", Indent No. 320, reveals that Nathaniel (Nathan) received on July 13, 1785, 4-11-5 sterling for militia duty as private. An article in *The State,* Columbia, South Carolina, October 3, 1904, stated that Nathan Evans received this sum for services "after the fall of Charleston." Evans, *Nathaniel Evans,* 15–17.
21. Evans, *Nathaniel Evans,* 37–45.
22. John Camden Hotten, *The Original Lists of Persons of Quality* (New York, 1874), 216.
23. Evans, *Nathaniel Evans,* 38–39.
24. Ibid., 40.
25. Ibid., 35.
26. Ibid., 37, 38, 40, 53.

Chapter II

1. Data gathered from the files of the United States Military Academy, West Point, New York.
2. Evans, *Nathaniel Evans,* 39.
3. Ibid., 38.
4. George F. Price, *Across the Continent with the Fifth Cavalry* (New York, 1883), 334; George W. Cullum, *Biographical Register of the Officers and Graduates of the United States Military Academy,* II, (New York, 1891), 365. Hereafter cited as Cullum, *Register.*
5. Cullum, *Register,* II, 208–366.
6. Price, *Across the Continent,* 344; Cullum, *Register,* II, 365.

7. Price, *Across the Continent*, 14, 334–335.

8. N. G. Evans, *Journal*. General Nathan George Evans's Private Papers in the possession of the Evans Family (hereafter cited as Evans Papers).

9. Ibid.

10. Ibid.

11. Ibid.

12. Price, *Across the Continent*, 335; Cullum, *Register*, II, 365; Evans Papers.

13. Price, *Across the Continent*, 335; [Letter] Chesley D. Evans to N. G. Evans, Marion, SC, May 14, 1856, Evans Papers.

14. Other officers of the 2nd Cavalry were Captains Earl Van Dorn, Edmund K. Smith, James Oakes, Innis N. Palmer, George Stoneman Jr., Theodore O'Hara, William R. Bradfute, Charles E. Travis, Albert G. Bracket, and Charles J. Whiting; 1st Lieutenants Richard W. Johnson, Joseph H. McArthur, Charles W. Field, Walter H. Jenifer, William H. Royal, Alexander H. Cross, William P. Chambliss, and Robert N. Eagles; 2nd Lieutenants John T. Shaaf, George B. Gosby, William W. Lowe, George Hartwell, Joseph F. Minter, Charles W. Phifer and Robert C. Wood, Jr., Price, *Across the Continent*, 26–28.

15. Among those who served with the two cavalry regiments were such men as Robert E. Lee, Albert Sidney Johnston, George B. McClellan, John Sedgwick, George H. Thomas, Edwin V. Sumner, John B. Hood, J.E.B. Stuart, Fitzhugh Lee, Earl Van Dorn, William H. Emory, Joseph E. Johnston, Edmund Kirby Smith, William J. Hardee, Nathan G. Evans, George N. Stewart, Eugene V. Crittenden, Andrew Jackson Jr., George Stonemen Jr., William D. DeSaussure, Kenner Garrard, Samuel D. Sturgis, and Innis N. Palmer. Price, *Across the Continent*, 22–27.

16. A. J. Long, *Memoirs of Robert E. Lee* (New York, 1886), 77.

17. O'Hara is the author of the often quoted poem "The Bivouac of the Dead."

18. Richard W. Johnson, *A Soldier's Reminiscences in Peace and War* (Philadelphia, 1886), 98.

19. Price, *Across the Continent*, 28–30, 335.

20. [Letter] I. Graham to N. G. Evans, Fort Leavenworth, (undated). Evans Papers. She is referring to Stuart's courtship of Miss Flora Cooke whom Stuart was soon to marry.

21. Johnson, *Reminiscences*, 101–102.

22. Price, *Across the Continent*, 32–34.

23. Johnson, *Reminiscences*, 101–102.

24. Evans Papers.

25. Douglas Southall Freeman, *R. E. Lee* (New York, 1934), I, 363.

26. Johnson, *Reminiscences*, 108.

27. Evans Papers.

28. Price, *Across the Continent*, 45; Freeman, Lee, I, 365–366. Freeman states that the command was composed of one company from Camp Cooper, one from Fort Mason, and two from Fort Chadbourne.

29. Price, *Across the Continent*, 45.

30. Ibid.

31. Evans Papers.

32. Price, *Across the Continent*, 45–49.

33. [LETTER] Lee to Evans, Fort Brown, Texas, August 15, 1856. Evans Papers.

34. [LETTER] Lee to Evans, San Antonio, Texas, August 3, 1857. Evans Papers.

35. [LETTER] Lee to Evans, San Antonio, Texas, August 25, 1857, Evans Papers.

36. [LETTER] Lee to Evans, San Antonio, Texas, August 28, 1857. Evans Papers.

37. [LETTER] Lee to Evans, San Antonio, Texas, September 15, 1857. Evans Papers.

38. Richard W. Johnson, *Memoir of Maj.-General George H. Thomas* (Philadelphia, 1881), 31.

39. *A Soldier's Honor by His Comrades with Reminiscences of Major-General Earl Van Dorn* (New York, 1902), 35; Price, *Across the Continent*, 68.

40. Johnson, *Reminiscences*, 119; Price, *Across the Continent*, 469.

41. *A Soldier's Honor*, 35; Price, *Across the Continent*, 68.

42. Price, *Across the Continent*, 69.

43. Marion *Star*, Marion, South Carolina, April 12, 1859.

44. Evans Papers. The flag and spoon are to be found in the South Carolina Room of the Confederate Museum, Richmond, Virginia.

45. Marion *Star*, April 12, 1859.

46. Price, *Across the Continent*, 70.

47. *A Soldier's Honor*, 37-38, quoting General Twiggs's Report, October 19, 1858.

48. Price, *Across the Continent*, 71, 335; *Reports and Resolutions of the General Assembly of South Carolina*, 1859, 541–542.

49. *A Soldier's Honor*, 40.

50. Price, *Across the Continent*, 335.

51. Marion *Star*, quoting Charleston *Courier*. Charleston, South Carolina; undated clipping in Evans Papers.

52. *Star* and *Courier*, Evans Papers.

53. *Star* and *Courier*, Evans Papers.
54. Marion *Star*, April 12, 1859.
55. Ibid.
56. Ibid.
57. Evans Papers.
58. Evans, *Nathaniel Evans*, 72.
59. *Reports and Resolutions of the General Assembly of South Carolina*, 1859, 541–42.
60. Evans Papers.
61. Evans, *Nathaniel Evans*, 74–78.
62. The groomsmen were Walker Adams, John Green, Chris Suber, Asa L. Evans, N. W. Rights Gist. Miss Gary chose as her attendants, Mrs. Emma Griffin, Susan Townsend, Emma Connor, Jennie Moseley, Mary McCall, and Mollie Peterkin. Evans Papers.

Chapter III

1. Evans Papers.
2. [LETTER] Mrs. N. E. Evans to Mrs. Mary Elizabeth Griffin, San Antonio, Texas, April 1861. Evans Papers.
3. Evans Papers.
4. [LETTER] Sarah Jane Evans to N. G. Evans, Marion, C.B., November 28, 1860. Evans Papers.
5. [LETTER] William Edwin Evans to N. G. Evans, Vera Cruz, Mexico, December 6, 1860. Evans Papers.
6. Evans, *Nathaniel Evans*, 51.
7. Recollections of the late George Clinton Evans, Sandersville, Georgia. Evans Papers.
8. Evans, *Nathaniel Evans*, 54.
9. Recollections of the late Mrs. N. G. Evans. Evans Papers.
10. Evans Papers.
11. Ibid.
12. Ibid.
13. *Official Records of the War of the Rebellion. A Compilation of the Official Records of the Union and Confederate Armies* (Washington, 1880–1901), Ser. I, Vol. 1, p. 33 (Hereafter cited as *OR*. All references are to Series I unless otherwise noted.) Evans was a major in the Confederate States Army.

14. Felix G. Defontaine, *Army Letters of "Personne,"* I (Columbia, South Carolina, 1896), 26.
15. [LETTER] Evans to his wife, Charleston, South Carolina, April 15, 1861. Evans Papers.
16. [LETTER] Evans to Mrs. Thomas R. Gary, Marion C.H., South Carolina, May 5, 1861. Evans Papers.
17. *OR*, IV, 1, 317.
18. [TELEGRAM] Francis W. Pickens to Evans, Charleston, South Carolina, May 16, 1861. Evans Papers.
19. [LETTER] Samuel Cooper to Evans, Montgomery, Alabama, May 20, 1861. Evans Papers.
20. Charleston *Mercury*, June 6, 1861.
21. Evans Papers.
22. [LETTER] Beauregard to Evans, Manassas Junction, Virginia, June 21, 1861. Evans Papers.
23. Evans Papers.
24. Eppa Hunton Jr., ed. *The Autobiography of Eppa Hunton* (Richmond, 1933), 29.

Chapter IV

1. *OR*, 2, 440–41.
2. James Longstreet, *From Manassas to Appomattox* (Philadelphia, 1903), 37–38.
3. Joseph E. Johnston, *Narrative of Military Operations* (New York, 1874), 33–39; *OR*, 2, 486–87.
4. Ibid., 40–41.
5. *OR*, 2, 326.
6. *OR*, 2, 487, 558–59; Johnston, *Narrative*, 41.
7. *OR*, 2, 487–88; Johnston, *Narrative*, 42.
8. Charleston *Mercury*, November 2, 1861; E. P. Alexander, *Military Memoirs of a Confederate* (New York, 1905), 30–31; Clarence Clough Ruel and Robert Underwood Johnson, editors, *Battles and Leaders of the Civil War*, 7 (New York, 1984–87), 185, hereafter cited as *Battles and Leaders*; *OR*, 2, 478, 559–60.
9. *OR*, 2, 560; *Battles and Leaders*, I, 185.
10. *OR*, 2, 559.
11. *The Daily Times*. Florence, S.C., March 6, 1915, quoting H. W. Brooker in the *State*, Columbia, 1915. A large number of Evans's men retreated in

other directions. His final loss was nineteen killed, one hundred and seventeen wounded, and eight missing. *OR*, 2, 566–67, 570.

12. Johnston, *Narrative*, 48–49.
13. *OR*, 2, 496; Edward A. Pollard, *The Lost Cause* (New York, 1866), 148.
14. Ibid.
15. *OR*, 2, 474, 477, 489, 490.
16. *OR*, 51, pt 1, 28, 31.
17. *Battles and Leaders*, I, 185.
18. Evans, *Nathaniel Evans*, 57.
19. Evans Papers.

Chapter V

1. *OR*, 51, pt 2, 191.
2. *OR*, 2, 1,000.
3. *OR*, 51, pt 2, 198-99; [LETTER] Thomas Jordan to N. G. Evans, Manassas, Virginia, July 26, 1861. Evans Papers.
4. [LETTER] R. E. Lee to N. G. Evans, Richmond, Virginia, July 26, 1861. Evans Papers.
5. Robert Stiles, *Four Years under Marse Robert* (New York, 1904), 59–60 (Shortly after their arrival in Virginia a number of the Mississippi troops fell ill with the measles.); Hunton, *Autobiography*, 45.
6. Ibid., 60, 64–65.
7. Evans, *Nathaniel Evans*, 38–39.
8. T. Campbell Copeland and Paul F. Mottelay, editors, *The Soldier in Our Civil War*, I, (New York, 1893), 148.
9. Stiles, *Four Years Under Marse Robert*, 61.
10. [LETTER] Beauregard to Evans, Fairfax C.H., Virginia, October 6, 1861. Evans Papers.
11. [LETTER] Beauregard to Evans, Fairfax C.H., Virginia, October 6, 1861. Evans Papers.
12. [LETTER] Beauregard to Evans, Fairfax C.H., Virginia, October 9, 1861. Evans Papers.
13. Hunton, *Autobiography*, 46; *OR*, 5, 347.
14. Ibid., 347.
15. Copeland and Mottelay et al., editors, *The Soldiers in Our Civil War*, I, 148.
16. *OR*, 5, 348-49; [LETTER] Beauregard to Evans, Centreville, Virginia, October 20, 1861. Evans Papers.
17. *OR*, 5, 349.

18. [LETTER] Beauregard to Evans, Centreville, Virginia, October 20, 1861. Evans Papers.
19. *OR*, 5, 290.
20. *OR*, 5, 293–95.
21. Evans Papers.
22. *OR*, 5, 363–64.
23. The same Jenifer who owned Gray Eagle.
24. *OR*, 5, 349.
25. *OR*, 5, 368–69.
26. *OR*, 5, 349.
27. Baker had disobeyed Stone's orders. Stone had instructed Baker to withdraw if he was opposed by a respectable force. Hunton, *Autobiography*, 48; *OR*, 5, 295–396, 300–301; 51, pt 1, 47.
28. Hunton, *Autobiography*, 48–50. Hunton maintains that it was 2:30 P.M. when he first sent White to Evans and 3:30 P.M. when he sent White the last time. Hunton was probably an hour late in his calculations. Evans states in his report that he sent the 18th Mississippi at 2:30 P.M., while Lt. Colonel Thomas M. Griffin states that the 18th Mississippi arrived at the scene of action about 2:30 P.M. *OR*, 5, 349, 365.
29. *OR*, 5, 297, 349. Wildman was not wounded in the charge that followed. Hunton, *Autobiography*, 56–57.
30. *OR*, 5, 349–50.
31. *OR*, 5, 297–98.
32. Hunton, *Autobiography*, 54–55; *OR*, 5, 361–62.
33. *OR*, 5, 350–52.
34. Felix G. DeFontaine ("Personne"), *Marginalia, or Gleanings From an Army Notebook* (Columbia, 1864), 103.
35. *OR*, 5, 333–34, 355; undated clippings in Evans Papers.
36. Hunton, *Autobiography*, 56, 57. Hunton states that Evans retired because he was afraid of a flanking movement up the Little River turnpike; *OR*, 5, 334, 350.
37. In examining the report more carefully it appears that 40 were killed, 113 wounded, and 2 missing. *OR*, 5, 308, 353.
38. *OR*, 5, 350.
39. [LETTER] Jordan to Evans, near Centreville, Virginia, October 22, 1861. Evans Papers.
40. "Kiawah" in Charleston *Mercury*, November 5, 1861; A. S. Salley, *South Carolina Troops in Confederate Service*, III, (Columbia, 1930), 73. Evans Papers. The same order (No. 47) published in *OR*, 5, 348, differs from the original in the following respects:

1. Left out "great" before "satisfaction."
2. "To the river" instead of "into Maryland."
3. "force of the enemy" instead of "Federal force."
4. "200 prisoners" instead of "520 prisoners."
5. "entitles" instead of "entitle."

41. Undated clippings in Evans Papers. Charleston *Mercury*, October 28, 1861.
42. Charleston *Mercury*, November 1, 1861.
43. Macon *Telegraph*, Macon, Georgia, undated, as quoted by Charleston *Mercury*, November 2, 1861. "Hermes" in Charleston *Mercury*, November 2, 1861. Howard Swiggett (ed.), *A Rebel War Clerk's Diary at the Confederate States Capital* by J. B. Jones, I (1935), 87.
44. *OR*, 51, pt 2, 414; "Personne" in Charleston *Daily Courier*, January 10, 1863; undated clippings. Evans Papers. General Stone was not as fortunate as Evans. The Federal reverse at Leesburg caused a great furor in the Federal Congress. The Northern losses were greatly exaggerated, but what caused the greatest consternation was the death of the renowned Baker. After some debate in both houses, Congress installed a committee to investigate the conduct of the war. This committee investigated the Leesburg affair and selected General Stone for the scapegoat. After a long investigation, Stone was imprisoned without being permitted to have a hearing or without being informed of the charges against him. He was released from prison on August 16, 1862, but it was not until February 27, 1863, that he appeared before the Committee on the Conduct of the War. This time Stone was furnished with a copy of the allegations against him and he promptly cleared himself. Stone returned to the army, but his persecution continued. This drove him to resign from the Federal service toward the close of the war. After his resignation was accepted, Stone went abroad, where he served many years with the distinction of chief of general staff to the Khedive of Egypt. James G. Blaine, *Twenty Years of Congress*, I, (Norwich, Connecticut, 1884), 378–95.
45. [LETTER] Gary to Evans, Bacon Race Church, Virginia, October 23, 1861. Evans Papers.
46. Recollections of the late Miss Mary Martin Evans, Edgefield, South Carolina; [LETTER] Gary to Mrs. Thomas R. Gary, Camp Butler, Virginia, October 30, 1861. Evans Papers.
47. *OR*, 5, 913–14.
48. *OR*, 5, 929–30.
49. *OR*, 5, 935, 945, 961.

50. *OR*, 5, 964; [LETTER] Beauregard to Evans, Centreville, Virginia, November 19, 1861. Evans Papers.

51. Recollections of former Governor John Gary Evans, Evans Papers; Dunbar Rowland (ed.), Jefferson Davis, *Constitutionalist, His Letters, Papers and Speeches*, V (New York, 1923), 175,177.

52. [LETTER] W. L. Featherston to Evans, Leesburg, Virginia, December 8, 1861. Evans Papers; [LETTER] W. L. Duff et al. to Evans, Leesburg, Virginia, December 8, 1861. Evans Papers.

53. Charleston *Mercury*, March 3, 1862.

54. *OR*, 5, 353–54.

55. [LETTER] A. G. Brown to Evans, Richmond, Virginia, April 4, 1862. Evans Papers.

Chapter VI

1. *OR*, 6, 347–48.

2. [LETTER] Evans to his wife, Adams' Run, South Carolina, December 23, 1861. Evans Papers.

3. [LETTER] William H. Gist to Evans, Union C.H., South Carolina, December 12, 1861. Evans Papers.

4. *OR*, 6, 354, 357, 359–61; 53, 202–3.

5. [LETTER] Evans to his wife, Adams' Run, South Carolina, January 17, 1862. Evans Papers.

6. *OR*, 6, 77–82.

7. [LETTER] Evans to his wife, Adams' Run, South Carolina, February 2, 1862. Evans Papers.

8. *OR*, 6, 89–90, 382.

9. *OR*, 6, 382.

10. *OR*, 6, 386.

11. Charleston *Daily Courier*, Charleston, South Carolina, February 15, 1862.

12. *OR*, 6, 391–93.

13. *OR*, 6, 395.

14. [LETTER] Evans to his wife, Adams' Run, South Carolina, February 20, 1862. Evans Papers.

15. [LETTER] Evans to his wife, Adams' Run, South Carolina, February 22, 1862. Evans Papers.

16. [LETTER] Evans to his wife, Adams' Run, South Carolina, March 2, 1862. Evans Papers.

17. [LETTER] Evans to his wife, Adams' Run, South Carolina, March 8, 1862. Evans Papers.

18. *OR,* 6, 400, 406–7.
19. [LETTER] Evans to his wife, Adams' Run, South Carolina, March 18, 1862. Evans Papers.
20. Evans Papers; Charleston *Daily Courier,* March 24, 1862.
21. [LETTER] Evans to his wife, Adams' Run, South Carolina, March 26, 1862. Evans Papers.
22. *OR,* 6, 113–19.
23. Charleston *Daily Courier,* April 5, 1862.
24. Chesley Daniel Evans, an officer in the home guard at Marion, later went to the front. Thomas Evans served the Confederacy as a purchasing agent, while Andrew Jackson Evans was bedridden. Charleston *Daily Courier,* April 8, 1862.
25. [LETTER] R. E. Lee to Evans, Richmond, Virginia, March 28, 1862. Evans Papers.
26. [LETTER] Lee to Evans, Richmond, Virginia, April 14, 1861. Evans Papers.
27. *OR,* 6, 247, 257–58, 263; 14, 13, 340.
28. *OR,* 14, 18–19.
29. *OR,* 14, 385.
30. Secessionville is situated on a peninsula on the east side of James Island, east of Fort Johnson.
31. *OR,* 14, 521–23.
32. *OR,* 14, 90–92, 566, 992. The part that Evans played in this battle is taken from his official report. Hagood states in his *Memoirs* that Evans's report is inaccurate and that the battle was an affair of outposts where the subordinate officers and troops engaged did the best they could under the circumstances. U. R. Brooks, ed., *Memoirs of the War of Secession: From the Original Manuscripts of Johnson Hagood* (Columbia, 1910), 97. See also Patrick Brennan, *Secessionville: Assault on Charleston* (Campbell, CA.: Savas Publishing Co., 1996).
33. *OR,* 14, 51, 91.
34. Brennan, *Secessionville,* 287–309.
35. *OR,* 14, 585.
36. *OR,* 14, 586.

Chapter VII

1. *OR,* 11, pt 3, 657. [LETTER] Evans to his wife, Richmond, Virginia, July 31, 1862. Evans Papers.

2. [LETTER] Evans to his wife, Richmond, Virginia, July 31, 1862. Evans Papers.
3. [LETTER] Evans to his wife, Laurel Hill near Richmond, August 10, 1862. Evans Papers.
4. *OR*, 11, pt 3, 657.
5. *OR*, 12, pt 2, 629–40.
6. *OR*, 12, pt 2, 628.
7. *OR*, 12, pt 2, 628–29.
8. *OR*, 12, pt 2, 627.
9. [LETTER] Evans to his wife near Leesburg, Virginia, September 4, 1862. Evans Papers.
10. [LETTER] Evans to his wife, near Leesburg, Virginia, September 4, 1862. Evans Papers.
11. John B. Hood, *Advance and Retreat, Personal Experiences in the United States and Confederate Armies* (Philadelphia, 1880), 38–39.
12. The Texans were much displeased over the arrest of Hood. As they passed Lee on their way up the mountain they began to shout for Hood. Lee sent for Hood and asked him to say that he regretted the occurrence, which Hood refused to do. After talking to Hood a little longer, Lee told Hood that he would suspend his arrest until after the forthcoming battle. Hood was never tried. Hood, *Advance and Retreat*, 39–40; J. B. Polley, *Hood's Texas Brigade, Its Marches, Its Battles, Its Achievements* (New York, 1910), 114–15.
13. *OR*, 19, pt 1, 939–42.
14. *OR*, 19, pt 1, 939.
15. *OR*, 12, pt 1, 939.
16. *OR*, 12, pt 1, 939–41.
17. *OR*, 12, pt 1, 143, 940. Evans's brigade lost 47 killed and 262 wounded in the Maryland campaign. Evans reported that his brigade had lost 1,024 out of 2,200 since July 30. *OR*, 12, pt 1, 811, 940.
18. [LETTER] Evans to his wife, Shepherdstown, Virginia, September 19, 1862. Evans Papers.
19. [LETTER] Evans to his wife, near Winchester, Virginia, September 29, 1862. Evans Papers.
20. [LETTER] Evans to his wife, near Winchester, Virginia, October 10, 1862. Evans Papers.
21. *OR*, 19, pt 2, 621, 674.
22. [LETTER] Evans to his wife, near Winchester, Virginia, October 18, 1862. Evans Papers.
23. *OR*, 19, pt 2, 683, 698.

24. [LETTER] Lafayette McLaws to N. G. Evans, Headquarters, 1st Division, Army of Northern Virginia, November 6, 1862. Evans Papers.
25. "Hermes" in *Tri-Weekly Mercury*, November 15, 1862.

Chapter VIII

1. [LETTER] W. F. Martin to A. L. Evans, Camp Vance near Hamilton, N.C., November 28, 1862. Evans Papers. *OR*, 18, 787.
2. [LETTER] Evans to his wife, Kinston, North Carolina, November 24, 1862. Evans Papers.
3. [LETTER] Evans to his wife, Kinston, North Carolina, December 5, 1862. Evans Papers.
4. *OR*, 18, 54–55.
5. "Personne" in the Charleston *Daily Courier*, January 5, 1862.
6. "Personne" in Charleston *Daily Courier*, January 5, 1862; OR, 18, 55, 113.
7. *OR*, 18, 55–56, 113.
8. "Personne" in Charleston *Daily Courier*, January 5, 1863.
9. *OR*, 18, 56, 113; "Personne" in Charleston *Daily Courier*, January 5, 1863.
10. "Personne" in Charleston *Daily Courier*, January 5, 1863; Charleston *Daily Courier*, December 17, 1862. "Personne" included the conversation in his article to give the public the true facts of the interview between Evans and Potter.
11. *OR*, 18, 56, 113; "Personne" in Charleston *Daily Courier*, January 5, 1863.
12. *OR*, 18, 112.
13. *OR*, 18, 56, 113.
14. *OR*, 18, 56–57, 121–22.
15. *OR*, 18, 117.
16. *OR*, 18, 117.
17. *OR*, 18, 57–58, 113–14, 117–19.
18. *OR*, 18, 60.
19. *OR*, 18, 112–14.
20. *Wilmington Journal*, December 18, 1862; January 8, 1863; Charleston *Daily Courier*, December 15, 17, 1862; January 9, 10, 15, 13, February 6, 1863.
21. Charleston *Daily Courier*, January 9, 1863.
22. Ibid.
23. *OR*, 18, 822, 855.
24. [LETTER] Evans to his wife, Kinston, North Carolina, December 25, 1862. Evans Papers.
25. Charleston *Daily Courier*, January 10, 1863.

26. [LETTER] T. D. Easton to Major ——, Charleston, South Carolina, February 14, 1863. Evans Papers.

27. Evans Papers.

28. Ibid.

29. [LETTER] T. D. Easton to Major ——, Charleston, South Carolina, February 14, 1863. Evans Papers.

30. Undated clipping. Evans Papers.

31. Charleston *Daily Courier*, February 23, 1863. Undated Clippings. Evans Papers.

32. [LETTER] Paul H. Hayne to Evans, Winnsboro, South Carolina, March 6, 1863. Evans Papers.

33. Due to the fall of Fort Donelson in the West and the inactivity of the Confederate Army in Virginia, the Southern people were very gloomy before the Confederate victory at Leesburg. Undated clippings. Evans Papers.

34. The original is in Evans Papers. There is also a printed copy of the poem in the Evans Papers, but it does not have the name of the newspaper or date.

35. [LETTER] A. G. Brown to Evans, Richmond, Virginia, February 27, 1863. Evans Papers.

36. [LETTER] A. G. Brown to Evans, Richmond, Virginia, February 27, 1863. Evans Papers.

37. Evans Papers.

38. [LETTER] Wm. Porcher Miles to Evans, Richmond, Virginia, March 4, 1863. Evans Papers.

39. [LETTER] John M. McQueen to Evans, Richmond, Virginia, March 15, 1863. Evans Papers.

40. *OR*, 18, 945. [LETTER] James L. Orr to Evans, Richmond, Virginia, April 9, 1863. Evans Papers.

41. Updated clipping. Evans Papers. The original petition is in Evans Papers.

42. Ibid.

43. *OR*, 18, 879, 893, 917, 977, 979, 1,011, 1,030, 1,041.

Chapter IX

1. [LETTER] Evans to his wife, Charleston, South Carolina, May 1, 1863. Evans Papers.

2. *OR*, 28, pt I, 67. [LETTER] Evans to his wife, Charleston, South Carolina, May 12, 1863. Evans Papers.

3. *OR*, 28, pt I, 67; [LETTER] Evans to his wife, Charleston, South Carolina, May 13, 1863. Evans Papers.

4. [LETTER] Evans to his wife, Montgomery, Alabama, May 24, 1863. Evans Papers.

5. Samuel N. Thomas Jr. and Jason H. Silverman, eds., *"A Rising Star of Promise": The Civil War Odyssey of David Jackson Logan, 17th South Carolina Volunteers, 1861-1864* (Campbell, CA: Savas Publishing Co., 1998), 95.

6. Smith Ketchen, "Smith Ketchen Diary While in the War, 1861-1865," *The Bulletin.* 13 (Chester District Genealogical Society, 1990), 69.

7. [LETTER] Evans to his wife, Jackson, Mississippi, May 29, 1863. Evans Papers.

8. [LETTER] Evans to his wife, Jackson, Mississippi, June 3, 1863. Evans Papers.

9. [LETTER] Evans to his wife, Jackson, Mississippi, June 3, 1863. Evans Papers.

10. [LETTER] Evans to his wife, Jackson, Mississippi, June 13, 1863. Evans Papers.

11. [LETTER] Evans to his wife, Jackson, Mississippi, June 17, 1863. Evans Papers.

12. [LETTER] Evans to his wife, Jackson, Mississippi, June 20, 1863. Evans Papers.

13. *OR,* 24, pt 3, 937, 945; [LETTER] Evans to his wife, Camp near Livingston, Mississippi, June 24, 1863. Evans Papers.

14. This difficulty with Evans was no doubt the reason that Johnston asked Beauregard to recall Evans. But due to the scarcity of troops at Charleston, Beauregard refused to comply with Johnston's request. *OR,* 28, pt 2, 173.

15. [LETTER] Evans to his wife, near Livingston, Mississippi, June 28, 1863. Evans Papers.

16. [LETTER] Evans to his wife, 25 miles from Vicksburg, Mississippi, July 2, 1863. Evans Papers.

17. [LETTER] Evans to his wife, 25 miles from Vicksburg, July 2, 1863. Evans Papers.

18. [LETTER] Evans to his wife, camp near Big Black Run, July 4, 1863. Evans Papers.

19. [LETTER] Evans to his wife, Jackson, Mississippi, July 14, 1863. Evans Papers.

20. [LETTER] Evans to his wife, Jackson, Mississippi, July 15, 1863. Evans Papers.

21. [LETTER] Evans to his wife, near Morton Depot, Mississippi, July 20, 1863. Evans Papers.

22. [LETTER] Evans to his wife, near Morton, Mississippi, July 22, 1863. Evans Papers.
23. [LETTER] Evans to his wife, near Morton, Mississippi, July 31, 1863. Evans Papers.
24. *OR*, 24, pt 3, 1043; 28, pt 2, 250.
25. [LETTER] Evans to his wife, Savannah, Georgia, August 8, 1863. Evans Papers.
26. *OR*, 28, pt 2, 259, 263.
27. *OR*, 28, pt 2, 265.
28. Evans Papers.
29. [LETTER] Evans to N. W. Gary, Charleston, South Carolina, September 5, 1863. Evans Papers.
30. *OR*, 28, pt 2, 306; [LETTER] Evans to his wife, Savannah, Georgia, August 26, 1863. Evans Papers.

Chapter X

1. *OR*, 28, pt 2, 309–10, 321.
2. Evans Papers.
3. [LETTER] Ripley to Evans, Charleston, South Carolina, September 12, 1863. Evans Papers.
4. [LETTER] Evans to Ripley, Mt. Pleasant, South Carolina, September 12, 1863. Copy, Evans Papers.
5. [LETTER] Evans to Thomas Jordan, Mt. Pleasant, South Carolina, September 14, 1863. Copy, Evans Papers.
6. Evans Papers.
7. [LETTER] Evans to Nance, Mt. Pleasant, South Carolina, September 15, 1863. Evans Papers.
8. [LETTER] Evans to Jordan, Mt. Pleasant, South Carolina, September 15, 1863; [LETTER] Evans to Jordan, September 20, 1862; [LETTER] Evans to Beauregard, Mt. Pleasant, South Carolina, September 20, 1863; [LETTER] Beauregard to Evans, Charleston, South Carolina, September 21, 1863. Evans Papers.
9. [LETTER] Evans to Beauregard, Mt. Pleasant, South Carolina, September 21, 1863. Copy, Evans Papers.
10. [LETTER] Ripley to Evans, Charleston, South Carolina, September 21, 1863; [LETTER] Evans to Ripley, Mt. Pleasant, South Carolina, September 25, 1863. Copy, Evans Papers.
11. [LETTER] Evans to Jordan, Mt. Pleasant, South Carolina, September 25, 1863. Copy, Evans Papers.

12. [LETTER] Evans to his wife, Mt. Pleasant, South Carolina, September 30, 1863. Evans Papers.
13. Evans Papers.
14. Ibid.
15. [LETTER] Evans to his wife, Mt. Pleasant, South Carolina, October 12, 1863. Evans Papers.
16. [LETTER] Evans to his wife, Mt. Pleasant, South Carolina, October 17, 1863. Evans Papers.
17. Charleston *Daily Courier*, November 4, 1863; [LETTER] Evans to his wife, Mt. Pleasant, South Carolina, November 4, 1863. Evans Papers.
18. [LETTER] Evans to his wife, Mt. Pleasant, South Carolina, November 4, 1863. Evans Papers.
19. [LETTER] G. W. C. Lee to Evans, Charleston, South Carolina, November 5, 1863. Evans Papers.
20. [LETTER] Evans to Lee, Mt. Pleasant, South Carolina, November 11, 1863. Evans Papers.
21. [LETTER] Evans to his wife, Mt. Pleasant, South Carolina, November 12, 1863. Evans Papers.
22. [LETTER] G. E. Pickett to Evans, Petersburg, Virginia, November 17, 1863. Evans Papers.
23. [LETTER] Evans to his wife, Mt. Pleasant, South Carolina, November 14, 1863. Evans Papers.
24. [LETTER] Evans to Jordan, Mt. Pleasant, South Carolina, November 24, 1863. Copy, Evans Papers. Copy of the charges in Evans Papers; *OR*, 28, pt 2, 583–84.
25. *OR*, 28. pt 2, 584–90.
26. *OR*, 28, pt 2, 583.
27. *OR*, 35, pt 1, 533.
28. *OR*, 35, pt 1, 543, 546.
29. *OR*, 35, pt 2, 347.
30. [LETTER] Evans to his wife, Mt. Pleasant, South Carolina, March 20, 1863. Evans Papers.
31. *OR*, 35, pt 2, 362.
32. *OR*, 35, pt 2, 369, 405.
33. [LETTER] Evans to his wife, Sullivan's Island, South Carolina, April 8, 1863. Evans Papers. *OR*, 35, pt 2, 369, 405.
34. *OR*, 35, pt 2, 425.
35. Charleston *Daily Courier*, April 18, 1864; *The Daily South Carolinian*, Columbia, South Carolina, April 19, 1864.
36. *OR*, 35, pt 2, 443.

Chapter XI

1. [LETTER] Wade Hampton to Evans, Columbia, South Carolina, April 19, 1863. Evans Papers.
2. [LETTER] Evans to Hampton, Charleston, South Carolina, April 22, 1863. Copy, Evans Papers.
3. [LETTER] T. D. Eason to Hampton, Charleston, South Carolina, April 20, 1863. Copy, Evans Papers.
4. The authors have been unable to find the pamphlet. [LETTER] Evans to McMaster, Mt. Pleasant, S.C., November 6, 1863. Evans Papers.
5. The *Daily South Carolinian*, Columbia, South Carolina, March 2, 1864. Most of the correspondence included in this article is to be found in Evans Papers.
6. Evans Papers.
7. Ibid.
8. [LETTER] W. W. Harllee et al to Evans, Marion, South Carolina, December 13, 1863. Evans Papers. This letter was not included in the *Daily South Carolinian*.
9. Evans Papers.
10. Ibid.

Chapter XII

1. [LETTER] B. D. Evans to N. G. Evans, In Bivouac, 2 miles East Marietta, Georgia, June 22, 1864. Evans Papers.
2. [LETTER] Evans to his wife, Petersburg, Virginia, October 7, 1864. Evans Papers.
3. Evans Papers; OR, 47, pt 2, 1,204.
4. Evans Papers; OR, 47, pt 2, 1,353.
5. Recollections of former Governor John Gary Evans.
6. [LETTER] M. E. Lomax to Evans, Midway, Alabama, September 16, 1867. Evans Papers.
7. [LETTER] Evans to his wife, Midway, Alabama, December 25, 1867. Evans Papers.
8. Evans, *Nathaniel Evans*, 57.
9. [LETTER] M. W. Gary to Mrs. Evans, Edgefield, South Carolina, November 31, 1868. Evans Papers.

BIBLIOGRAPHY

Manuscripts

General George Nathan Evans Papers
Lieutenant David Jackson Logan Papers

Primary Documents

Memorandum of Staff Officers of the Confederate States Army. n.p., n.d.
South Carolina, Reports and Resolutions of the General Assembly of South Carolina, 1859.
Southern Historical Society Papers, 1892.
Special Orders of the Adjutant and Inspector-General's Office, Confederate States, 1861. n.p., n.d.
The War of the Rebellion: A Compilation of the Official Records of the Union and Confederate Armies. Gettysburg, PA: The National Historical Society, 1972.

Primary Sources

A Soldier's Honor by His Comrades with Reminiscences of Major-General Earl Van Dorn. New York, 1902.
Alexander, E. P. *Military Memoirs of a Confederate.* New York, 1908.
Brooks, U. R., ed. *Memoirs of the War of Secession: From the Original Manuscript of Johnson Hagood.* Columbia, 1910.
Buel, Clarence Clough and Robert Underwood Johnson. *Battles and Leaders of the Civil War.* 4 vols. New York, 1884–1887.
DeFontaine, Felix G., *Marginalia or Gleaning from an Army Notebook.* Columbia, 1864.

_____. *Army Letters of 'Personne.'* 5 vols. Columbia, 1896–1897.

Evans, Clement A., ed. *Confederate Military History.* 12 vols. Atlanta, 1899.

Ford, Arthur Peronneau. *Life in the Confederate Army; Being Personal Experiences of a Private Soldier in the Confederate Army.* Washington, DC: The Neal Publishing Co., 1905.

Hood, John B. *Advance and Retreat, Personal Experiences in the United States and Confederate Armies.* New Orleans, 1880.

Hudson, Joshua Hilary. *Sketches and Reminiscences.* Columbia, SC: The State Co., 1903.

Jervey, Theodore Dehon. *Charleston During the Civil War.* Washington, DC: [private printing], 1915.

Johnson, John. *The Defense of Charleston Harbor, Including Fort Sumter and the Adjacent Islands, 1863-1865.* Charleston, SC: Walker, Evans & Cogswell Co., 1890.

Johnson, Richard. *A Soldier's Reminiscences in Peace and War.* Philadelphia, 1886.

Johnston, Joseph E., *Narrative of Military Operations.* New York, 1874.

Jones, Samuel. *The Siege of Charleston and the Operations on the South Atlantic Coast in the War Among the States.* New York: The Neale Publishing Co., 1911.

Ketchen, Smith. "Smith Ketchen Diary While in the War, 1861–1865," *The Bulletin.* 13 [Chester District Genealogical Society, 1990] 8–15, 64–71, 96–103, 128–135.

Longstreet, James. *From Manassas to Appomattox.* Philadelphia, 1903.

Mackintosh, Robert Harley Jr. *"Dear Martha ...": The Confederate War Letters of a South Carolina Soldier, Alexander Faulkner Fewell.* Columbia, SC: The R. L. Bryan Company, 1976.

Pollard, Edward A. *The Lost Cause.* New York, 1866.

Ripley, Warren. *Siege Train: The Journal of a Confederate Artilleryman in the Defense of Charleston.* Columbia, SC: University of South Carolina Press, 1986.

Roman, Alfred. *The Military Operations of General Beauregard.* 2 vols. New York, 1883.

Stevens, Robert J. *Captain Bill.* Richburg, SC: The Chester District Genealogical Society, 1985.

Twiggs, H. D. D. "The Defense of Battery Wagner," *Southern Historical Society Papers.* 20 (1892) 166–183.

Newspapers

Charleston *Daily Courier*, 1858–1865.
Charleston *Mercury*, 1858–1865.
Daily South Carolinian, Columbia, SC, 1864.
Daily Times, Florence, SC, 1915.
Marion Star, Marion, SC, 1859.
The State, Columbia, SC, 1902.
Tri-Weekly Mercury, Charleston, SC, 1862–1863.
Wilmington Journal, Wilmington, NC, 1862–1863.

Secondary Sources

Amann, William Frayne. *Personnel of the Civil War*. New York: T. Yoseloff, 1961.

Barefoot, Daniel W. *General Robert F. Hoke: Lee's Modest Warrior*. Winston-Salem: John F. Blair, Publisher, 1996.

Bearss, Edwin C. *The Vicksburg Campaign*. Dayton, OH: Private Printing, 1986.

Beers, Henry Putney. *The Confederacy: A Guide to the Archives of the Government of the Confederate States of America*. Washington, DC: National Archives and Records Administration, 1986.

Benedict, David. *History of the Baptist Denomination in America*. 2 vols. Boston, 1913.

Bettersworth, John K. *Confederate Mississippi: The People and Policies of a Cotton State in Time of War*. Baton Rouge: Louisiana State University Press, 1943.

Black, Robert C. III. *The Railroads of the Confederacy*. Chapel Hill: University of North Carolina Press, 1952.

Boucher, Chauncey Samuel. *The Nullification Controversy in South Carolina*. Chicago, 1916.

Bradshaw, Timothy Jr., *Battery Wagner: The Siege, The Men Who Fought, and The Casualties*. Columbia, SC: Palmetto Historical Works, 1993.

Brennan, Patrick. *Secessionville: Assault on Charleston*. Campbell, CA: Savas Publishing Company, 1996.

Burton, E. Milby. *The Siege of Charleston, 1861-1865*. Columbia, SC: University of South Carolina Press, 1971.

Cauthen, Charles E. *South Carolina Goes to War, 1860-1865*. Chapel Hill: University of North Carolina Press, 1950.

Cavanaugh, Michael and William Marvel. *The Petersburg Campaign: The*

Battle of the Crater – "The Horrid Pit," June 25–August 6, 1864.
Lynchburg, VA: H. E. Howard, 1989.

Cisco, Walter Brian. *States Rights Gist: A South Carolina General of the Civil War.* Shippensburg, PA: White Mane Publishing Company, Inc., 1991.

Clark, Walter, ed. *Histories of the Several Regiments and Battalions from North Carolina in the Great War, 1861–1865.* Wendell, NC: Broadfoot's Bookmark, 1982.

Crawford, Samuel W. *The Genesis of the Civil War: The Story of Sumter.* New York, 1887.

Cullen, Joseph P. *The Peninsula Campaign, 1862: McClellan and Lee Struggle for Richmond.* Harrisburg, PA: Stackpole Books, 1973.

Cullum, George W. *Biographical Register of the Officers and Graduates of The United States Military Academy.* 7 vols. New York, 1901.

Current, Richard E., ed. *The Encyclopedia of the Confederacy.* 4 vols. NY: Simon & Schuster, 1993.

Davies, John. *A History of Wales.* London: Penguin Books, 1993.

Davis, Nora M. "Jefferson Davis' Route from Richmond, Virginia, to Irwinville, Georgia, April 2-May 10, 1865." *The Proceedings of the South Carolina Historical Association.* Columbia, 1941.

_____. *Military and Naval Operations in South Carolina, 1860-1865: Chronological List, With Reference to Sources of Further Information.* Columbia, SC: South Carolina Archives Department, 1959.

Davis, William C. *The Battle of Bull Run.* Garden City, NY: Doubleday and Company, Inc., 1977.

_____. *The Image of War, 1861-1865: The Embattled Confederacy.* Garden City, NY: Doubleday & Company, Inc., 1982.

_____. *The Image of War, 1861-1865: The Guns of '62.* Garden City, NY: Doubleday & Company, Inc., 1982.

Eaton, Clement. *A History of the Old South.* Prospect Heights, IL: Waveland Press, 1975.

Edwards, Morgan. "Materials Towards a History of the Baptists in Delaware State." vol. [part] III. *Pennsylvania Magazine of History and Biography.* IX. Philadelphia, 1885.

Ellsworth, Eliot Jr. *West Point in the Confederacy.* NY: G. A. Baker & Co., 1941.

Evans, James Daniel. *History of Nathaniel Evans and His Descendants.* Columbia, 1904.

Foner, Eric. *A Short History of Reconstruction.* NY: Harper & Row, Publishers, 1990.

Fonvielle, Chris E. Jr. *Last Rays of Departing Hope: The Wilmington Campaign.* Campbell, CA: Savas Publishing Company, 1997.

Ford, Lacy K. Jr. *Origins of Southern Radicalism: The South Carolina Upcountry, 1800-1860.* NY: Oxford University Press, 1988.

Freeman, Douglas S. *R. E. Lee.* 4 vols. New York, 1934.

_____. *Lee's Lieutenants: A Study in Command.* 3 vols. NY: Charles Scribner's Sons, 1942–1944.

Gallagher, Gary, ed. *The Fredericksburg Campaign.* Chapel Hill: University of North Carolina Press, 1996.

Gregg, Alexander. *History of the Old Cheraws.* Columbia, 1905.

Grimsley, David A. *Battles in Culpepper County, 1861-1865.* Culpepper, VA: Exponent Printing Office, 1900.

Hennessy, John. *The First Battle of Manassas: An End to Innocence.* Lynchburg, VA: H. E. Howard, 1989.

_____. *Return to Bull Run: The Battle and Campaign of Second Manassas.* NY: Simon and Schuster, 1993.

Holzman, Robert S. *Stormy Ben Butler.* NY: Macmillan, 1954.

Hope, W. Martin and Jason H. Silverman. *Relief and Reconstruction in Post-Civil War South Carolina: A Death by Inches.* Lewiston, NY: The Edwin Mellen Press, 1997.

Hotten, John Camden. *The Original Lists of Persons of Quality.* New York, 1874.

Howe, Thomas J. *The Petersburg Campaign: Wasted Valor, June 15-18, 1864.* Lynchburg, VA: H. E. Howard, 1988.

Johnson, Richard W. *Memoir of Maj.-General George H. Thomas.* Philadelphia, 1881.

Johnston, R. M. *Bull Run: Its Strategy and Tactics.* New York, 1913.

Johnston, William Preston. *The Life of Albert Sidney Johnston, Embracing His Services in the Armies of the United States, the Republic of Texas, and the Confederate States.* New York, 1879.

Jones, William. *Christ in Camp: Religion in the Confederate Army.* Harrisonburg, PA: Sprinkle Publications, 1986.

Jordan, Weymouth T. Jr., comp. *North Carolina Troops, 1861-1865, A Roster.* Raleigh, NC: North Carolina Division of Archives and History, 1975.

Kinard, Jeff. *The Battle of the Crater.* Fort Worth, TX: Ryan Place Publishers, 1954.

Klein, Maury. *Days of Defiance: Sumter, Secession, and the Coming of the Civil War.* NY: Alfred A. Knopf, 1997.

Krick, Robert K. *Stonewall Jackson at Cedar Mountain.* Chapel Hill: University of North Carolina Press, 1990.

Lee, Fitz Hugh. *General Lee.* New York, 1894.

Long, A. J. *Memoirs of Robert E. Lee.* New York, 1886.

Long, E. B. *The Civil War Day by Day: An Almanac, 1861-1865.* Garden City, NY: Doubleday & Company, Inc., 1971.

Lonn, Ella. *Desertion During the Civil War.* Gloucester, MA: Peter Smith, Inc., 1966.

Martin, David G. *The Second Bull Run Campaign.* Conshohocken, PA: Combined Books, Inc., 1997.

Massey, Mary Elizabeth. *Ersatz in the Confederacy.* Columbia: University of South Carolina Press, 1952.

Matter, William D. *If It Takes All Summer: The Battle of Spotsylvania.* Chapel Hill: University of North Carolina Press, 1988.

McPherson, James M. *For Cause & Comrades: Why Men Fought in the Civil War.* NY: Oxford University Press, 1997.

Merrill, James M. "Notes on the Yankee Blockade of the South Atlantic Seaboard, 1861-1865," *Civil War History* (December 1958) 387-397.

Meyer, Jack Allen. *South Carolina in the Mexican War: A History of the Palmetto Regiment of Volunteers, 1846-1917.* Columbia: SC Department of Archives and History, 1996.

Miers, Earl S. *The Web of Victory: Grant at Vicksburg.* Baton Rouge: Louisiana State University Press, 1984.

Miller, Francis Trevelyan. *The Photographic History of the Civil War: Forts and Artillery.* New York: Castle Books, 1957.

Moore, Albert. *Conscription and Conflict in the Confederacy.* NY: Hillary House, 1963.

Newton, Steven H. *The Battle of Seven Pines.* Lynchburg, VA: H. E. Howard, 1993.

Page, Thomas Nelson. *Robert E. Lee.* New York, 1911.

The Pocotaligo Expedition: Southwestern South Carolina, October 21-23, 1862. Montmorenci, SC: Western Carolina Historical Research, 1997.

Price, George F. *Across the Continent with the Fifth Cavalry.* New York, 1883.

Rhea, Gordon. *The Battle of the Wilderness.* Baton Rouge: Louisiana State University Press, 1995.

_____. *The Battle of Spotsylvania Court House.* Baton Rouge: Louisiana State University Press, 1997.

Robertson, James I. Jr. *Soldiers Blue and Gray.* Columbia, SC: University of South Carolina Press, 1988.

Salley, A. S. *South Carolina Troops in Confederate Service.* Columbia, SC: The R. L. Bryan Co., 1913.

Sears, Stephen. *To The Gates of Richmond: The Peninsula Campaign.* NY: Ticknor & Fields, 1992.

Sifakis, Stewart. *Compendium of The Confederate Armies: North Carolina.* NY: Facts on File, 1992.

_____. *Compendium of The Confederate Armies: South Carolina and Georgia.* NY: Facts on File, 1995.

_____. *Who was Who in the Civil War.* NY: Facts on File Publications, 1988.

Steere, Edward. *The Wilderness Campaign: The Meeting of Grant and Lee.* Mechanicsburg, PA: Stackpole Books, 1994.

Swanberg, W. A. *First Blood: The Story of Fort Sumter.* NY: Scribners, 1957.

Tanner, Robert G. *Stonewall in the Valley: Thomas J. "Stonewall" Jackson's Shenandoah Valley Campaign, Spring 1962.* Garden City, NY: Doubleday & Company, 1976.

Tenney, W. J. *The Military and Naval History of the Rebellion in the United States.* New York, 1865.

Thomas, Samuel N. Jr. and Paul C. Whitesides. *Under the Leaves of the Palmetto: York County's Confederate Veterans.* York, SC: Historical Center of York County, 1994.

_____. *The Dye is Cast: The Scots-Irish and Revolution in the Carolina Back Country.* Columbia, SC: Palmetto Conservation Foundation, 1996.

_____. and Jason H. Silverman. *"A Rising Star of Promise": The Civil War Odyssey of David Jackson Logan, 17th South Carolina Volunteers, 1861-1864.* Campbell, CA: Savas Publishing Company, 1998.

_____. *Jefferson Davis in South Carolina.* Columbia, SC: Palmetto Conservation Foundation, 1998.

Trotter, William R. *Ironclads and Columbiads: The Civil War in North Carolina, The Coast.* Winston-Salem, NC: John F. Blair, 1989.

Trudeau, Noah Andre. *Bloody Roads South: The Wilderness to Cold Harbor, May–June 1864.* Boston: Little, Brown & Co., 1989.

Utley, Robert M. *The Indian Frontier of the American West, 1846-1890.* Albuquerque: University of New Mexico Press, 1984.

Walker, Peter F. *Vicksburg: A People at War, 1860–1865.* Chapel Hill: University of North Carolina Press, 1960.

Warner, Ezra J. *Generals in Gray: Lives of the Confederate Commanders.* Baton Rouge: Louisiana State University Press, 1959.

Wert, Jeffry D. *General James Longstreet: The Confederacy's Most Controversial Soldier: A Biography.* NY: Simon & Schuster, 1993.

Wheeler, Richard. *On Fields of Fury: From The Wilderness to The Crater: An Eyewitness History.* NY: HarperCollins, 1991.

Wiley, Bell Irvin. *The Life of Johnny Reb: The Common Soldier of the Confederacy.* Baton Rouge: Louisiana State University Press, 1993.

Williams, T. Harry. *P.G.T. Beauregard: Napoleon in Gray.* Baton Rouge: Louisiana State University Press, 1955.

Wise, Stephen R. *Gate of Hell: Charleston, 1863.* Columbia: University of South Carolina Press, 1995.

Young, James C. *Marse Robert.* New York, 1929.

INDEX